Cambridge Topics in Geography: second series

*Editors*   Alan R. H. Baker, Emmanuel College, Cambridge
Colin Evans, King's College School, Wimbledon

# Planned development in the socialist world

## Graham Smith

Lecturer in Geography, University of Cambridge

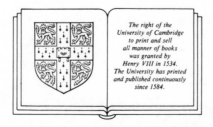

The right of the
University of Cambridge
to print and sell
all manner of books
was granted by
Henry VIII in 1534.
The University has printed
and published continuously
since 1584.

## Cambridge University Press

Cambridge
New York   Port Chester   Melbourne   Sydney

Published by the Press Syndicate of the University of Cambridge
The Pitt Building, Trumpington Street, Cambridge CB2 1RP
40 West 20th Street, New York, NY 10011, USA
10 Stamford Road, Oakleigh, Melbourne 3166, Australia

First published 1989

Printed in Great Britain at the University Press, Cambridge

*British Library cataloguing in publication data*
Smith, Graham, *1953–*
   Planned development in the socialist world.
   – (Cambridge topics in geography. Second series)
   1. Soviet Union. Regional planning
   I. Title
   36.6'0947

*Library of Congress cataloging in publication data*
Smith, Graham, 1953–
   Planned development in the socialist world / Graham Smith.
   106 p. 25.5 cm. – (Cambridge topics in geography. Second series)
Bibliography: p. 103
Includes index.
1. Central planning–Soviet Union. 2. Soviet Union–Economic
policy-1917– 3. Soviet Union–Social conditions-1917- I. Title.
II. Series.
HC335.S5369 1989
338.947--dc19                          88-37373
                                           CIP

ISBN 0 521 30546 2 hard covers
ISBN 0 521 26946 6 paperback

**Acknowledgements**
The author and publishers would like to thank the following for
permission to reproduce photographs:
Novostii Press (pages 40, 55, 56, 79, 87, 99)
David King (page 21)

# Contents

# Preface

The countries which make up the socialist or 'second' world are of vital importance to understanding the modern world in which we live. Yet in comparison with geographical studies of the 'first' and 'third' worlds, the socialist world has received little attention. This book is a contribution to rectifying this imbalance by providing an introduction to the social and economic development of the socialist world and to the Soviet Union in particular. The book is written for geographers, although those also embarking upon the study of economics or politics should find it of value. It departs in two ways from usual geographical approaches to the countries of the socialist world. Firstly, it is not a traditional regional geography textbook in which regions are described and analysed. Rather, it latches onto the theme of planned development and attempts to show in both an historical and a systematic way, how various strategies of development are conceived and how they are bound up with the territorial organisation of society and with the nature of regions, cities and the countryside and with the lives of the people who inhabit these places. Secondly, this book is not concerned with the technicalities of the Plan or only with the impact that its translation into practice has on the space-economy. Instead, planned development is interpreted as being part of an unfolding historical and political process, in which the changing territorial structure of society is the focus, and the role of vested interest groups provides much of the key to an understanding of development.

Rather than attempt to deal with the experiences of a large number of socialist states in the short space available, this work concentrates on the Soviet Union. Such a focus can be easily justified given the Soviet Union's significance as the first country to introduce socialist planning, and the pivotal role that planned development has played in making it a superpower. The experiences of other socialist countries, however, are not neglected. Chapter 1 deals with alternative development strategies in other socialist countries, notably China, Kampuchea and Hungary, and compares these experiences with that of the Soviet Union. In chapter 2, particular attention is paid to the neglected geographical study of the Stalinist model of development which I argue produced a geography of combined and uneven development which is of crucial importance to understanding the territorial organisation of modern Soviet society and the problems it now faces. In chapters 3 to 6, the various aspects of contemporary development are examined systematically – urbanisation and urban problems, regional policy and development, the economic and social development of the USSR's non-Russian periphery, and rural development. This should make it easier for the reader to make interesting comparisons with particular countries in both the developed and the developing world.

The first part of this book was written at the University of Cambridge, and it was completed during sabbatical leave at the University of California, Los Angeles. I am pleased to acknowledge the help provided by the library staff at both institutions for making the task of writing this book even more pleasurable. I am also grateful to the editors of the series, Alan Baker and Colin Evans, for their encouragement and comments, and to Ian Agnew and Ian Gulley for drawing the maps and diagrams. Lastly and most importantly, I thank Marilyn and Alexander for their patience. This book is dedicated to them.

Graham Smith
Sidney Sussex College, Cambridge

# 1 Socialism and development

Winston Churchill once described the Soviet Union as 'a riddle wrapped in a mystery inside an enigma'. The objective of this book is to show that a socialist society like the Soviet Union, although defying the type of generalisations that can be made about Western-type societies, need not remain a puzzle. The book is organised around the theme of planned development, a major feature of socialist societies, and one which is central to understanding much of their human geographies. It is a theme which is inextricably bound up with the territorial organisation of such societies and with the way in which territorial planning affects the character of their regions, cities and countryside and the lives of the peoples who inhabit these places.

Vital to understanding the geography of planned development is the role played by the state, which is of far more significance in determining the territorial organisation of society than in non-socialist countries. It is the state – more specifically its political elites – whose actions largely determine the nature of socio-economic development and its resultant impact on places. Yet as we shall see, the decisions that political elites make do not occur in a decision-making vacuum; they are also a product of a variety of constraints and experiential circumstances which has often led to different strategies of development. Moreover, although socialist countries are characterised by a highly centralised one-party state, we cannot fully comprehend the nature of the developmental strategies adopted by those in power and the logic behind their decisions without acknowledging that even in the most authoritarian state, major interest groups, with vested interests, play an important part in the making of such decisions. We will therefore have much to say about the role of industrial managers, urban planners, regional and local interests, environmental concerns, and the like, in influencing the course of planned development.

This book focuses on the Soviet Union, the first and historically the most important of the socialist world countries. Arguably too it is the nearest to the archetypal case of socialist development. Where appropriate, comparisons will also be made with other socialist countries as well as with the non-socialist world.

## What is the socialist world?

What then is the socialist world, which states does it include, and why? Our task is not made any easier by the prolific increase in the number of states since the early 1960s under some form of socialist or Marxist-Leninist rule. Then, the world political map would have contained fourteen generally recognised socialist states, the Soviet Union and its East European allies (German Democratic Republic, Czechoslovakia, Poland, Hungary, Bulgaria, Romania, Yugoslavia and Albania), China,

Mongolia, North Korea, North Vietnam and Cuba. By the mid-1980s membership of this world had grown to include South Vietnam, Laos, Kampuchea, Afghanistan and Nicaragua, and a number of other countries, mostly in Africa, many of whose designation as 'a socialist state' is more contentious. Defined in terms of their self-identification with Marxism-Leninism and the interpretation of that doctrine in the light of their own history and culture, there are perhaps around forty socialist states making up over half of the world's population (Fig. 1.1).

Closer scrutiny of the socialist world reveals that it no longer represents a cohesive body of states. A quarter of a century ago, the dozen or so socialist countries then in existence represented a geographical extension of the 'Soviet model' from which they generally claimed to have derived their inspiration, and in which, as in Eastern Europe, they owed their existence. Most were founding members of the two Soviet-dominated international organisations, the Warsaw Pact and the Council for Mutual Economic Assistance (CMEA or Comecon). Today the socialist world no longer represents a united geopolitical bloc on the world stage. The Chinese-Soviet split in the late 1950s, which most commentators would acknowledge heralded one of the most significant chapters in the history of the socialist world, was followed by Albania leaving both the Warsaw Pact and Comecon, and Albania in turn breaking publicly with China. Relations between wayward Yugoslavia and the Soviet Union remain strained, while Romania, the maverick state of Eastern Europe, has increasingly adopted a critical stance towards the Soviet Union. Besides periodic

Fig. 1.1   The socialist world.

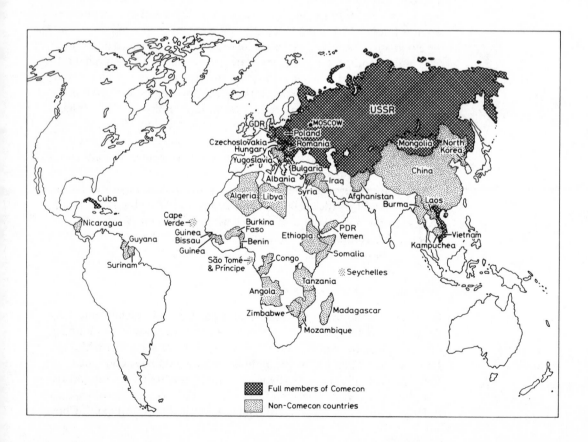

skirmishes on the Chinese-Soviet border, the socialist world has also experienced some of the most bloody and protracted wars of recent times – between China and Vietnam, and between Vietnam and Kampuchea. Similarly, the adoption of several ideological variants or strategies for development has destroyed the neat one-time notion of a monolithic world in which the Soviet model was the only path to follow. In increasing numbers, countries have been developing their own programmes for development to suit their special circumstances.

The increasing plurality of the socialist world therefore makes it more difficult to identify what makes this world different, other than the fact that such countries label themselves as socialist. As our primary concern is to identify a socialist world within which we can locate and compare the Soviet developmental experience, it is more useful to single out more 'objective' characteristics which appear to bear a more direct relationship to the essentials of Marxism-Leninism. Three such distinguishing features of socialist states can be identified: a commitment to Marxism-Leninism, extensive state ownership, and central planning. No claim is made that countries meeting such criteria can be clearly distinguished from non-socialist countries. For example, a number of West European states practise a high degree of state ownership and central planning but would clearly not claim to be socialist. Nor is it being suggested that these are the only criteria for identifying the parameters of the socialist world. What we are suggesting though is that we will be better placed to draw a distinction between socialist and non-socialist (capitalist) countries.

### Commitment to Marxism-Leninism

Socialist states are guided in their actions by the principles of 'scientific socialism' as originally set out by the nineteenth-century philosophers, Karl Marx and Friedrich Engels, and as developed by the Russian revolutionary and statesman, Vladimir Illyich Lenin. In their aim of constructing a programme for a better society, it was to be the task of a socialist state to work towards the fullest possible satisfaction of society's material and cultural needs, leading ultimately to the universal goal of Full Communism. For such societies, the term 'development' is therefore understood as inextricably bound up and informed by a particular set of beliefs and aims as developed by Marx, Engels and Lenin, and as modified by subsequent indigenous thinkers to fit their particular socio-economic and historical circumstances. It signifies nothing short of the total territorial transformation of society leading to the eradication of social inequality and injustice. Such a programme contains four explicit aims, each of which has important geographical implications. Firstly, it entails the 'gradual abolition of the distinction between town and country'. This sweeping phrase of Engels is predicated on the social inequalities which are reflected in divisions of labour between town and countryside. It thus becomes part of the project of socialism to remove such spatial and class inequalities characteristic of capitalism. Secondly, an ending to inter-regional inequalities is envisaged. This is to be achieved by a more even distribution of both economic activity and population throughout the country, and by singling out the more backward regions for special treatment. Thirdly, through an explicit policy of socio-economic development, socialism envisages removing the social inequalities and injustices which separate ethnic communities, and which is especially important to multinational societies like China, the Soviet Union and Yugoslavia. Finally, it entails the explicit goal of harnessing nature in a planned and controlled way so that the environment will be utilised for the betterment of humanity. No state in the socialist world would as yet lay claim to having fully achieved such broad aims. It is for this reason that caution should be exercised in labelling socialist countries as 'communist'.

## Extensive state ownership

An important hallmark of socialist countries is the extent to which the state has control over territorial ownership of the means of production and over the management of resources. Territorial ownership of the means of production here means ownership of major resources within its territory which are central to production and to economic and social development. This includes land, capital and technology. The state also has control over 'things' which are not thought of immediately as 'resources', such as income, education and social status. To a far greater extent than in non-socialist countries, the state can thus determine how resources are to be allocated and which regions, cities and neighbourhoods are to receive priority in their distribution, and who within these places are to benefit. There is, however, considerable variation in state policy towards state ownership. As Table 1.1 shows, some socialist regimes have less direct control over the means of production, and have purposely retained private ownership in some sectors of their economies. For example, in Poland, nearly four-fifths of agricultural land is in private hands in contrast to many other socialist countries where the state possesses a virtual monopoly over its ownership and management. All socialist states, however, play a far more pivotal role in economic and social life than their non-socialist counterparts and it is precisely because of this that the prime agent in the developmental process is the state.

**Table 1.1  Share of the state-owned (socialist) sector in selected socialist countries**

| Country | Percentage of national income | Percentage of industry | Percentage of agriculture |
|---|---|---|---|
| USSR | 100.0 | 100.0 | 100.0 |
| Bulgaria | 99.9 | 99.8 | 99.9 |
| Hungary | 97.6 | 99.3 | 98.9 |
| German Dem. Rep. | 96.4 | 97.9 | 95.5 |
| Mongolia | 100.0 | 100.0 | 99.9 |
| Poland | 84.4 | 98.0 | 22.7 |
| Romania | 95.5 | 99.7 | 85.6 |
| Czechoslovakia | 99.5 | 100.0 | 97.6 |
| Cuba | n.a. | 100.0 | 77.6 |

n.a. = not available
*Source:* S. White (1983) 'What is a communist system?' *Studies in Comparative Communism* 16(4), p. 256.

## Central planning

The national economies of the socialist world are variously referred to as 'centrally planned economies', 'command economies', or less frequently and inappropriately as 'Soviet-type economies'. All imply that central planning is of fundamental importance. Ownership of the means of production enables the state to plan the territorial allocation and distribution of resources in a forward-thinking way and on a scale unmatched by non-socialist countries. Through a series of national, regional and city plans, targets are set for allocating resources and fulfilling set production targets, and for providing the necessary social goods and services for the years ahead. In organising its resources in this way, central planning enables the state to decide what proportion of total production is to be reinvested and in what sectors of the economy, the amount which is to be earmarked for social consumption, and how much is to be allocated to every district, city and region. In short, central planning enables its political elites to affect the nature of development at all geographical levels in society.

It will now be apparent that development means something different to socialist societies than it does to non-socialist countries. For socialist countries it is inextricably bound up with the very ideology of socialism and of creating a more just society. The conduct of development also differs. Unlike non-socialist countries, development is inseparable from the state and the planning process. We can therefore define planned development as a process giving rise to the thorough reorganisation of society based on the centrally controlled allocation and management of resources and justified on the grounds of working towards the socialist goals of a fairer and more equitable society.

## The myth of the socialist monolith

The above criteria stress the uniqueness of the socialist world; yet uniqueness does not imply uniformity. Making sense of planned development also means acknowledging the geographical diversity of the socialist world, for it is this very diversity which helps us to understand the adoption and implementation of very different strategies for development.

Three such sources of geographical diversity can be singled out. Firstly, there is the *context* within which socialism is established. It is important to acknowledge that socialist states came into existence in a variety of very different societies. It is therefore important to recognise the role that the following socio-economic and political factors play in structuring the process of a society's development:

(a)  cultural heritage
(b)  natural resource endowment
(c)  the structure of society (agrarian or industrial)
(d)  multiethnic character
(e)  degree of integration into the world economy
(f)  political relations with other states, particularly with its neighbours.

Secondly, there is the *form* of socialism adopted. Various labels have been applied to socialist countries which reflect the adoption of very different brands of socialism: 'Maoist', 'Titoist', 'Leninist'. Each ideology has a quite different effect on the way in which society is organised. Compare, for instance, Yugoslavia and the Soviet Union. In the former, the territorial organisation of the economy is decentralised; political and economic power in what is often characterised as 'Tito's road to socialism' became highly devolved, and each industrial enterprise – based on workers' cooperatives – was to have a considerable amount of autonomy in the running of its economic affairs. Contrast this with a strong centrally administered Leninist ideology – characteristic of the Soviet Union – where the centre has control over producers who are directly accountable to detailed directives from the centre.

Finally, there is the *level* of development which a socialist country has reached. As Table 1.2 shows, socialist countries are found at all levels of development. They include some of the poorest countries in the world (e.g. Ethiopia, Kampuchea, Mozambique) as well as some of the most industrialised (e.g. Soviet Union, North Korea, Hungary, GDR). In short, the socialist world has its own 'first' and 'third' worlds, which has a parallel with 'the Western world' in its division between the more developed European countries and those of the less developed continents of Africa and Asia. Such levels of development have also mapped out a geography of dependent development in which the poorer are highly dependent on the socialist world's global (China, USSR) and regional (Vietnam, Cuba) 'superpowers' for economic aid and technical assistance. It is a geography of dependent development which is also bound up with socialist superpowers maintaining regional

**Table 1.2   Indices of socio-economic development for selected socialist countries**

|  | Population mid-1985 (millions) | Urbanisation 1985 (% of population living in cities) | GNP per caput 1985 (US dollars) | Life expectancy at birth 1985 (years) |
|---|---|---|---|---|
| Soviet Union | 277.4 | 66 | — | 70 |
| Czechoslovakia | 15.5 | 66 | — | 70 |
| German Democratic Republic | 16.6 | 76 | — | 59 |
| Hungary | 10.6 | 55 | 1,950 | 71 |
| Poland | 37.2 | 60 | 2,050 | 72 |
| China | 1,040.3 | 22 | 310 | 69 |
| Laos | 3.6 | 15 | — | 45 |
| North Korea | 20.4 | 63 | — | 68 |
| Vietnam | 61.7 | 20 | — | 65 |
| Angola | 8.8 | 25 | — | 44 |
| Ethiopia | 42.3 | 15 | 110 | 45 |
| Mozambique | 13.8 | 19 | 160 | 47 |
| Tanzania | 22.2 | 14 | 290 | 52 |
| Cuba | 10.1 | 71 | — | 77 |
| Nicaragua | 3.3 | 56 | 770 | 59 |

*Source:* World Bank (1987) *World Development Report 1987* Oxford University Press, Oxford, pp. 202–3, 266.

spheres of influence against encroachment by the capitalist world and in some instances by each other.

## Territorial strategies for development

The adoption of a wide range of developmental strategies is both a reflection and a product of the socialist world's diversity. They vary from the urban-industrial bias of the Soviet Union and Eastern Europe to the rural emphasis of China and Tanzania. They are also a consequence of *conscious decisions* made by political elites within the context of the circumstances that we have outlined above. Such routes for development should not be viewed as part of a well-thought-through 'grand strategy'; more often than not, they are a consequence of decisions of the moment. Nor is the means for achieving such transformations universal. In the Soviet Union and Kampuchea, it involved the use of violence in order to effect change. As other experiences show, as in China and Tanzania, the process of rapid transformation need not involve large-scale violence and human suffering.

Four main developmental strategies can be identified. All are explicitly territorial strategies for they involve redefining relations between town and country and between regions. Also, countries have often moved from one developmental strategy to another in accordance with the changing political, economic and social circumstances in which they find themselves.

### 1   Balanced development/limited urbanisation

This strategy is rural in orientation and attempts to ensure a balanced development between town and countryside. Consequently, urbanisation is kept in check and the countryside is singled out for special treatment. The clearest example of this type is China from the Great Leap Forward to the death of Mao Zedong (1958–76). Other examples would include the Soviet Union during the period of its so-called New Economic Policy (1921–28), Cuba (1962–65) and Albania (1965–85).

By far the most original and outstanding example is that of China. The task facing post-revolutionary China was daunting and what it has achieved the more impressive. With 20 percent of the world's population to support, it has managed without any significant external assistance to provide adequate food and other basic needs for its one billion people. It has also managed to transform its society from abject poverty through industrialisation without undergoing rapid urbanisation. In spite of high levels of national economic growth, only 22 percent of the population were living in cities in 1987 compared with 10 percent in the 1950s. How then are we to explain this apparent anti-urban bias? Certainly the pre-revolutionary relationship of the countryside to the city and the way in which successive waves of urban elites exploited the peasantry over centuries is of significance. The politico-administrative cities of ancient and feudal China, populated by corrupt bureaucrats and administrators, lived on the wealth exacted from the peasantry through taxation. Then there were the more recently established commercial cities inhabited by merchants and 'middle men' who exploited the peasantry through trade and financial manipulation. Finally, there were the nineteenth-century foreign-dominated 'treaty ports' of the Western imperial powers, who extracted the resource wealth of the countryside largely for export abroad. It was such historical circumstances in a country whose 1949 Revolution was peasant-based and peasant-led which were to play a decisive part in formulating China's subsequent pattern of development.

It was not, however, until the 'Great Leap Forward' of the late 1950s that China based its path to development on the countryside and introduced policies which were to keep the urban growth of its largest cities in check. Complementing such a policy was a desire to strike a proper balance between the more urbanised and relatively prosperous coastal areas and the rural and impoverished interior. In essence, it involved a policy of industrial deconcentration and of urbanising the countryside, in which the rural commune was to play a significant part. This basic social unit, formed by 1958 as a result of the collectivisation of land, was designed to meet the essential needs of its members on the principle of self-reliance while at the same time creating a rural society based on justice and equality. Through state financing, small rural and medium-scale regional industries were introduced to service the peasant consumers of the commune, to produce the necessary 'inputs' for agriculture (fertilisers, electricity, machine tools), and to process local resources and rural produce. This helped the agricultural sector to modernise quickly.

Such a policy of deconcentration did not however stop 'the flight from the countryside'. Consequently, from 1958 onwards, restrictions were imposed on change of residence, especially from the countryside to the cities. In addition, a series of migration programmes were introduced to encourage reverse migration. Between 1958 and 1960, as part of a campaign to reclaim wasteland for agricultural cultivation, a substantial number of urban middle-class students were encouraged to resettle in the countryside. Some 53,000 of these students were sent from the more urbanised province of Honan to Tsinghai. Other campaigns followed; during the 1960s and early 1970s, for instance, some 17 million people left the cities. In Shanghai alone, between 1968 and 1976, some 1.3 million inhabitants left for the countryside. These schemes were not without their problems, but increased state investment in rural services and infrastructural facilities did help to make rural resettlement more palatable.

Considerable advances have also been made in reducing the urban-rural gap in health and education, in part due to state policy in diverting resources from city to countryside. Yet in spite of rural industrialisation and tightly controlled rural-to-urban migration, it would be misleading to label China's development strategy as simply one of rural bias. Industry continued to receive priority over agriculture and most of this industrial investment occurred in the cities. In the period under review, industry received around 50 percent of all capital investment; and most industrial output came from the cities. These developments notwithstanding, what is most striking is that China managed to strike a balance between town and country development, and in the process has avoided large-scale urban growth and city unemployment which plague so many third world countries.

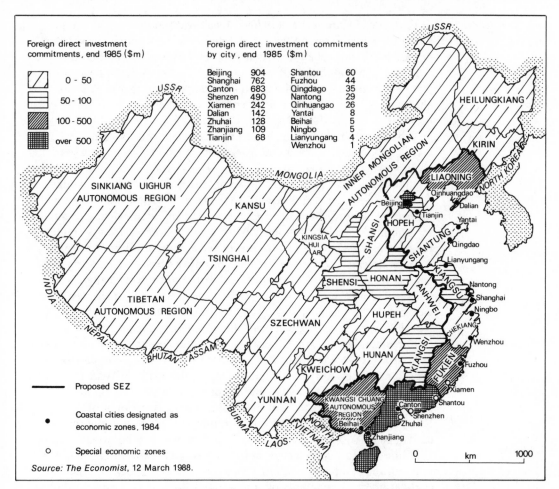

Fig. 1.2 China's Special
Economic Zones (SEZs).

Since the late 1970s, however, a clear change in the state's
development strategy is apparent. The 'open door' policies of the New
Chinese Socialism have paved the way to certain pressures, familiar to
other third world countries, which act to reinforce resource allocations
towards large cities. In 1984, some of the largest coastal cities were
granted special economic privileges, which seem to contradict the time-
hallowed policy favouring the development of smaller, inland cities. In
an attempt to hasten the 'modernisation of the Chinese economy', this
policy places emphasis squarely on promotion of foreign trade. In
1988, this was extended and now all the coastline is a giant Special
Economic Zone (SEZ) (Fig. 1.2). The idea is based on the notion that
by stimulating investment in these large cities, economic benefits will
'trickle down' to smaller settlements. It is however a pattern of
development which instead may threaten to reinforce the schism
between the rural hinterland and the coastal cities, and stimulate the
urban growth of large cities and the country's greater dependency on
outside capital.

## 2  Uneven development/deurbanisation

This is the most self-evident of the strategies of rural bias for it
represents a policy of purposely starving the city of investment and of
engineering the reduction of urban inhabitants. The most extreme case

of this type is Kampuchea (1975–78), as vividly portrayed in David Putnam's award-winning film, *The Killing Fields*. Kampuchea's urban population had reached its height just before the 1975 Revolution; one year later the population of its primate city, Phnom Penh, declined from an estimated 2.5 million to as low as perhaps 50,000. A similar although not quite so dramatic trend could be seen in South Vietnam between 1975 and 1980.

Urban growth in Kampuchea's immediate pre-revolutionary years was largely created by a booming wartime economy associated with neighbouring American involvement in the Vietnam War, and by the immigration of rural migrants escaping guerrilla warfare and famine. According to Murray and Szelenyi (1984), it was these conditions of 'overurbanisation' which were to precipitate and ideologically to guide the Kampuchean Revolutionary Movement, the *Khmer Rouge*, under the fanatical leadership of Pol Pot, to seize upon a policy of purposely running down the cities (deurbanisation) as the basis for building a new socialist society. As they put it, 'Deurbanisation typically . . . is a response to an "overheated" boom in urban economy which went along with the excessive exploitation of the countryside'. To the Revolutionary Kampucheans with their support base in the countryside, the differences between town and country could not have been more self-evident. The city had been built up as a consequence of French and later American capital. During the Vietnam War, the USA had considerable geostrategic and economic interests tied up in prosperous Phnom Penh. Yet the countryside and the bulk of Kampucheans benefited little and continued to suffer considerable hardships made worse by periodic famine and by US bombing expeditions into Kampuchean border areas. Deurbanisation, then, was to entail the complete rebuilding of Kampuchean society and the eradication of all remnants of colonial and Western influence, including the city. It was a strategy which entailed the emptying of the cities and urban labour was forced to work in various irrigation and reclamation schemes as part of a programme to rebuild an agrarian society. The totalitarian methods used resulted in the death of an estimated two million Kampucheans.

With the Vietnamese occupation of Kampuchea and the defeat of Pol Pot, a degree of normality has returned to social life. It would also seem that Kampuchea is beginning a new phase of limited urban growth. Resettlement in the cities is being encouraged but the devastation caused by 'the terror' has left cities like Phnom Penh without basic public utilities and services. Whether Kampuchea's countryside can sustain a growing urban population while the country has only a limited integration in the world economy, remains to be seen.

### 3 Uneven development/urban industrialisation

There is another strand of socialist thought which interprets the city in a positive light and which views urbanisation as bound up with building socialism. Lenin interpreted the meaning of urbanisation in the writings of Marx and Engels as an important precondition for the Soviet Union's economic and social development. Accordingly, 'the cities represent the centres of economic, political, and spiritual life of the people and are the main forces of progress' (1963: vol. 23, 341). It was the city which was to lead the countryside and it was the progressive forces of urbanisation which were given the responsibility of destroying the backwardness and archaic traditions of the countryside which made up what Engels called 'the idiocy of rural life'. It was this urban orientation in combination with a programme of rapid industrialisation, most clearly associated with the economic development of Stalin's Russia (1928–53), and the export of this developmental model to Eastern Europe (1945–53), which were to transform these predominantly rural societies into urban industrialised countries at rates unrivalled by the industrialising experiences of the non-socialist world.

This model of extensive growth is based upon the development of heavy industries – steel, coal, electricity, heavy engineering and other defence-related industries – which receive the lion's share of state investment. Other sectors of the national economy are neglected, notably agriculture and light manufacturing industry. Investment in housing and in the provision of both urban and rural services and amenities is also assigned low priority. Yet even with large inputs of capital, rapid industrialisation would not be possible without the absorption of an extremely large pool of industrial labour. Given the low proportion of urban dwellers, industry has to rely on the countryside for its labour force. As industrial investment is city based, the outcome is a large flow of labour from rural to urban areas. This rapid growth model is also accompanied by a concentration of capital investment expenditures in the largest urban agglomerations in order to maximise industrial output and returns on investment. Consequently, it is these cities which experience the fastest growth in industrial employment and population.

It is therefore a strategy of uneven development in which particular cities receive priority over smaller towns and the countryside. Yet the unconstrained growth of large urban agglomerations is viewed as undesirable from the perspectives of building a more equitable society. Measures like restricting residence in large cities are introduced and schemes to control new industrial development in large cities are employed. The inability of city authorities to house the growing influx of migrants also necessitates the introduction of these measures. The preoccupation with rapid economic growth, however, and the accompanying need for a large supply of labour in order to meet the requirements of extensive industrialisation, means that policies of deconcentration and of striking a more equitable balance between settlements and regions have limited impact on altering spatial imbalances.

## 4   Intensive development/slower urbanisation

The countries which have gone through the model described above now make up the most urbanised and industrialised members of the socialist world. For the Soviet Union and other industrialised countries like Hungary and Czechoslovakia, the era of fast urban growth and rapid industrialisation has ended. Far greater consideration is now being given to more balanced development, both sectorally (between heavy industry, light manufacturing and agriculture), and spatially (between town and countryside). This also reflects the greater emphasis given by state spending to improving overall living standards, particularly of the more backward regions and smaller settlements.

Hungary is a good example. From the early 1960s onwards, an effort has been made to stimulate the social and economic development of its regions and settlements as a counterweight to the industrial and demographic growth of the country's primate city, Budapest. In the period of post-war reconstruction (1945–53), Budapest continued to dominate the Hungarian economy. By the mid-1950s, its share of total industrial output stood at 42.2 percent, with 44.1 percent of the industrial workforce living there. Throughout this period, primarily as a result of continuing industrial investment in the city, its urban growth continued; by 1960, 18.1 percent of Hungary's population were living in the capital city compared with 17.3 percent in 1949. From the early 1960s onwards, however, a radical policy of decentralisation was introduced to relieve the pressure on Budapest; it included measures to restrict the city's industrial and demographic growth, the most far-reaching of which was the removal of industrial plants employing 20,000 or more workers from the city and their relocation elsewhere in the country. Other measures have included investing more in rural and small-town social infrastructure, including housing.

While such measures have not stopped the growth of industrial employment in Budapest, they have contributed to slowing down its rate of urban growth and improving the quality of life for those living outside the capital city. As in the other industrialised socialist countries, decision-takers are also trying to move away from a reliance on large inputs of capital and labour for city-based industrial growth, towards a more modern and efficient economy which relies on technological innovation and higher labour productivity.

It is this very strategy – of moving from 'extensive industrialisation' to 'intensive development' – which forms a cornerstone to Gorbachev's programme for restructuring the Soviet economy. This policy of *perestroika* (or 'restructuring'), introduced in 1986, calls for available resources and investment capital to be more effectively used for the modernisation of urban industry and for the establishment of high-technology industries. As labour is to be used more productively and industry and the urban service sector are to be run more efficiently, it is envisaged that there will no longer be the same need for a large urban labour force. One possible consequence of such a change in policy will be to help reduce the continuing migration of labour into large cities which at present find it difficult to cope with the extra demands for housing and other urban services and amenities. We will return to this model of intensive development in later chapters.

## The state, interest groups and development

So far we have treated the state, specifically its political elites, as a monolithic force in the adoption of particular developmental strategies. In reality those involved in the politics of development do not constitute an undifferentiated mass. Rather a variety of powerful interest groups exist which have vested interests in promoting particular policies. The amount of power that these interest groups have at their disposal differs between socialist countries as it does with a country's changing government. Interest groups also vary in the degree to which they can influence outcomes. Yet if we are to understand fully the nature and patterns of development in the socialist world, we must also address ourselves to this important aspect.

The most commonly used set of models to understand the Soviet political decision-making process is pluralistic in nature. The models are based on the assumption that Soviet society, like capitalist democracies, is made up of a socially varied population and that these social differences reflect conflicts of group interest. There is, however, one vital difference between the two types of political system: power is more politically and territorially centralised in socialist countries. This clearly has important implications for the range of interest groups who are permitted by the state to participate formally in the decision-making process and who can influence outcomes. At the height of Stalin's power (1928–53), for instance, interest groups were not permitted to exist; the arena of political decision-making was confined to the top echelons of the party-state system. Disagreement was not permitted and strict conformity to central dictats became the norm. Those with alternative views became victims of the system. Over the past thirty years, however, power has become more fragmented and as a consequence a disparate number of interest groups can have an influence in the lobbying, formulation and implementation of developmental policies. But interest groups are sanctioned by the party-state which means that it is really only those groups which make up the party-state and bureaucratic apparatus who have some input into the decision-making process. So when Hough (1972:28) argues that politics in the Soviet Union revolves around 'conflict among a complex set of crosscutting and shifting alliances of persons with divergent interests', what he is also saying is that such policy conflicts are confined to the legitimate organisational channels of the party-state and bureaucratic apparatus. Within this arena, interest groups constitute self-interested institutions, able and willing to promote their own policies and vested interests. For those social groupings excluded from the party-state apparatus and who make up the ordinary population, there is little opportunity for interest-group articulation.

Many of the interest groups which we will be most concerned with are territorially based. The immensity of Soviet territory (it is two and a half times the size of the USA!) has meant that Moscow requires fifteen union republics (see Fig. 5.1), more than a hundred regionally based administrative organisations, and more than 40,000 local governments (*soviets* or councils) to administer and run the affairs of society. So the centre may wield considerable control, but it is physically impossible for it to control and supervise everything. Regions and localities therefore do have some leeway in managing their own affairs provided that they conduct their actions within the guidelines and directives sent down by Moscow. They also, quite naturally, have their own territorial interests to safeguard which may bring them into conflict with central interests. This is particularly so with issues of resource allocation in which regional and local authorities are involved in safeguarding and in promoting their particular interests. Territorially based institutions therefore attempt to influence outcomes which favour their particular institutions and the

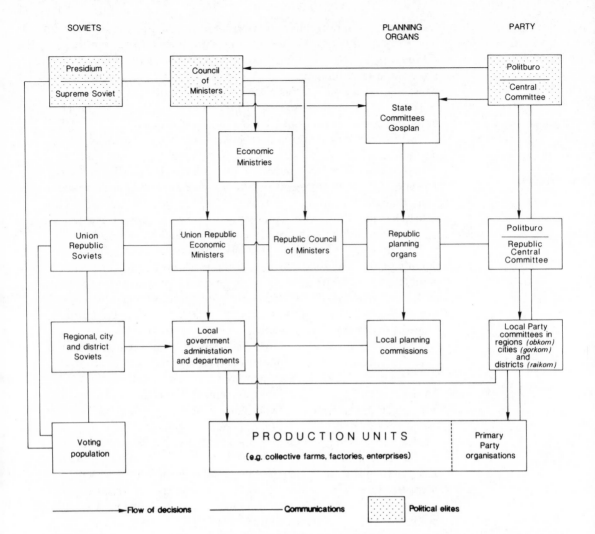

Fig. 1.3 A simplified view of
the Soviet political and
economic system.

territories they represent. In short, territorial politics have come to play
an important part in socialist development.

Figure 1.3 illustrates the complexity of the Soviet political and
economic system. To simplify matters, for the purposes of the theme of
this book, we can identify three types of interest group.

## 1 Political elites

Incumbents at the very apex of the party-state decision-making process
constitute the political elites. It is this grouping which is responsible for
setting the policy agenda and for determining priorities in terms of the
allocation and distribution of resources. It is the personalities and
alliances, and the factional politics which they represent, which make
this pinnacle of the Soviet system interesting to Western political
analysts. There are changing alliances between those favouring rapid-
or slow-growth policies; between those who advocate more spending on
the country's defence and those favouring more spending on housing
and consumer welfare; between those who favour investing in regions
where national growth is maximised and those concerned with more
balanced regional development; and between proponents of particular
development schemes and those opposed to them.

In issues of development and resource allocation we can make a distinction between two further types of interest group, both of which are institutionally based. Although both types form an integral part of the party-state and bureaucratic apparatus, their distinctiveness springs from the centrally and territorially organised nature of the country's political, administrative and economic systems. We can distinguish between the central planners and the economic ministries on the one hand and territorially based authorities on the other hand.

## 2  The central planners and economic ministries

The dominance of central planning and of economic management in issues of development are the consequence of the significance of central planners and the economic ministries in the organisation of the planning process. It is, however, important to distinguish between them. At the heart of central planning is *Gosplan*, The State Committee for Planning. It has responsibility for coordinating the planning process and has analogous committees at the republican, regional and local levels. *Gosplan* has no independent authority and is strictly accountable to the Politburo. It is *Gosplan*'s function to translate the development priorities set out by the Politburo into plan instructions for the economic ministries. It is these *economic ministries* which are responsible for the management of the national economy. Each ministry is in charge of a specific sector of economic activity (e.g. ministries of agriculture, coal, iron and steel, transport, construction) and for the particular units of production (e.g. factories, enterprises, farms) within its jurisdiction. More or less all the ministries responsible for industry are entirely centralised, while some other ministries, particularly those concerned with social welfare (e.g. education, health) have counterparts in the fifteen union republics. While some ministries wield more weight than others (the heavy and defence industries in particular), all are engaged in pressing the interests and problems of their industry upon the central planners.

One important outcome of the planning process is that due primarily to the continuing reliance on the branch principle in administering the economy, sectoral planning inevitably takes priority over questions of regional and local development. One highly detailed account of the planning process highlights such a feature: out of 203 steps in compiling a ministry's plan, the regional dimension is introduced only at step 179, after most of the key decisions about allocation have been made. Moreover, the regional part of the plan is not binding on the ministry; it represents desirable but not obligatory targets for regional development. Economic ministries then tend to behave according to their own interests, investing and developing projects in those places which maximise returns. Nor does the planning system help encourage ministries to coordinate in the interests of particular places. Thus ministries may build factories but skimp on the housing needed to find and keep an adequate labour force. But it may also be in the interests of a particular ministry to champion regional interests (e.g. the Ministry of Oil in backing the development of oil-rich Western Siberia).

### 3 Territorially-based institutional groupings

This includes representative party and state or soviet organs at the union republics, regional, district and city levels. In many respects they make for strange bedfellows. On the one hand there are the territorial organs of the Communist Party whose main functions are to direct and oversee the Plan and to ensure its fulfilment. As a highly centralised and bureaucratised organisation, each party committee is strictly subordinate to its immediate higher authority. But directives often allow for local interpretation which gives the party a degree of flexibility. As the eyes and ears of the centre, it also provides an important function of feedback on problems associated with resource allocation or in the implementation of particular decisions. In many respects the local and regional party organisations are caught between ensuring that central policy is carried out and that additional resources can be obtained for their region or locality from the centre. The role of the local party has often been described as 'mediator' in its attempt to resolve conflicts that inevitably arise between representatives of particular local interests and the centre. The local party is in effect often pushed into the role of balancing the competing demands which arise as part of the politics of development.

On the other hand, there are the locally-elected *soviets* (councils) and their various departments. These parallel the Communist Party in their existence at all geographical scales. Their functions vary but generally they are there to serve the interests of the local community and to provide a range of services not dissimilar to local governments in Western countries. Due primarily to the role that the local party plays in the selection of candidates for election to the soviets and the veto it possesses over appointments to key full-time positions in the various departments of the soviets, the soviets' activities are heavily circumscribed by the local party organisation. But what often unites local soviet and party organisations are mutual local interests.

The rest of this book takes up particular perspectives on the planned development of the Soviet Union. We begin by examining in chapter 2 the Stalinist model of development as it unfolded in the most formative period of Soviet planning (1928–53). It was to have a profound and lasting impact on the territorial organisation of society and so it is necessary to understand this model before we can grasp many of the economic and social problems facing today's Soviet Union. The subsequent chapters are contemporary in focus. Chapter 3 examines the impact of the Soviet pattern of urbanisation and the consequences that it has had for the social and economic life of the city. Chapter 4 focuses on the regions and the particular developmental strategies and policies which have been pursued. In chapter 5 we consider the USSR's non-Russian regions and how centrally engineered social and economic development has affected these communities. Finally, chapter 6 takes up the theme of rural development; the impact of particular regional development projects is examined as is the territorial organisation of production and the problems the countryside now faces in relation to central planning and control.

# 2  The Stalinist model for development

In spite of inheriting an economy at an early stage of development, the Soviet Union came into existence on an advantageous footing compared with other socialist countries. Firstly, from its tsarist predecessor it acquired an Empire which had already established the foundations of an urban-industrial economy. Industrialisation, which did not get under way until the closing decades of the nineteenth century, had begun the process of mapping out an era of prosperity for the national economy. By the eve of the First World War, the Russian Empire was producing more steel and machinery than either France or the Austrian Empire and was a major exporter of a number of agricultural products, notably of wheat. Secondly, post-revolutionary Russia was different from other socialist countries in its extraordinarily rich reserves of natural resources and fossil fuels. These included large deposits of coal, iron ore, gold, platinum and oil. Before the 1917 Russian Revolution, it was primarily the vast resources of the most heavily populated and industrialised part of the country, European Russia, which were serving the economy's needs (Fig. 2.1); however, what this region had to offer was nothing in comparison to the as yet largely unrealised richness of Siberia. Finally, the Empire also bequeathed to its successor state a rapidly expanding modern railway network which had done much to expedite the supply of necessary resources to the country's industrial heartlands of Moscow, St Petersburg, the Donbass and the Baltic regions. This contribution of 60,000 kilometres of railway to the greater integration of the national economy had reached its pre-revolutionary apogee by 1911 with completion of the Trans-Siberian Railway connecting Moscow with the Pacific Coast.

Such apparent economic progress, however, masked a society riddled with all the hallmarks of underdevelopment. Firstly, the new Soviet state inherited a rural society *par excellence*. Just over four-fifths of the population eked out a meagre rural existence based largely on archaic and inefficient farming practices, and illiteracy was high. This contrasted with Britain which, having completed its industrial revolution some decades before, had over four-fifths of its population living in cities. Figures on urbanisation for European Russia show that the city population had grown considerably during the latter half of the nineteenth century, primarily as a result of migration from the countryside (Table 2.1). Yet on the eve of the Revolution, just four cities accounted for around one-third of the total population (Moscow, St Petersburg, Kiev and Odessa). Elsewhere, in Siberia and Central Asia, industrialisation had made little headway. This new urban and primarily European labour force was also largely unskilled and unaccustomed to the runnings of a modern factory economy.

Secondly, the urban-industrial development that had taken place was

Fig. 2.1 The industrial development of European Russia in 1914.

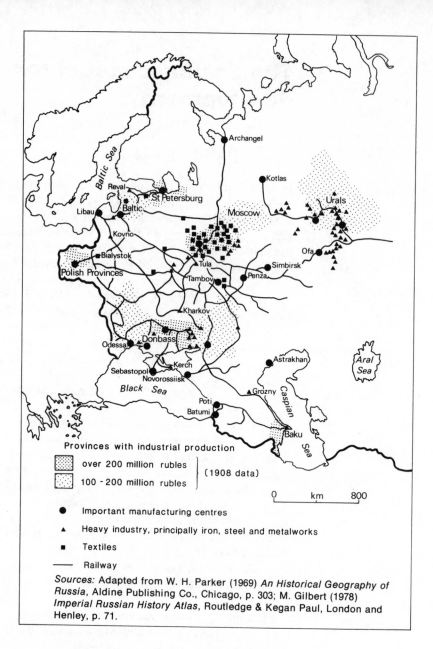

Fig. 2.1 The industrial development of European Russia in 1914.

Provinces with industrial production

- over 200 million rubles ⎫
- 100 - 200 million rubles ⎬ (1908 data)

● Important manufacturing centres

▲ Heavy industry, principally iron, steel and metalworks

■ Textiles

— Railway

*Sources:* Adapted from W. H. Parker (1969) *An Historical Geography of Russia*, Aldine Publishing Co., Chicago, p. 303; M. Gilbert (1978) *Imperial Russian History Atlas*, Routledge & Kegan Paul, London and Henley, p. 71.

### Table 2.1 The urban population of European Russia, 1811–1914

| Year | Millions | % of total population |
|------|----------|-----------------------|
| 1811 | 2.77 | 6.6 |
| 1863 | 6.15 | 10.0 |
| 1897 | 12.05 | 12.9 |
| 1914 | 18.60 | 15.3 |

*Source:* A. G. Rashin (1956) *Naselenie Rossii za 100 let*, Moscow, p. 98.

partly dependent on financial support from overseas European investors. German and French capital, in particular, provided much of the finance for capital equipment and infrastructural development. For example, in the Donbass, which by 1900 accounted for more than half the Russian iron smelting, only one of its nine blast furnaces was wholly Russian-owned, and more than half of its coal mines were under Franco-Belgian ownership. Russia then was not only dependent on exporting agricultural products and raw materials in order to accumulate the necessary capital for industrialisation but, in addition, a significantly large proportion of finance for industrial development came directly from foreign capital. The country's further industrialisation was therefore financially and economically heavily dependent on, and tied to, a world economy.

For the newly established socialist state, the questions of industrialisation and economic progress were bound up with securing a socialist society. What was central therefore was how the poor, backward and unequal society which it had inherited was to become a fully industrialised state. How was industrialisation to be achieved and at what level of disruption to its society? This chapter begins by examining these questions as debated by the architects of the new state and its leading thinkers during the 1920s. These debates provide us with an insight into the range of developmental strategies open to the Soviet Union. Next, we examine the actual model of development adopted and its impact on the territorial reorganisation of society.

## The industrialisation debate

One of the major issues to dominate the question of development during the 1920s was where the resources for Russia's industrialisation were to come from. In the early 1920s, when Soviet expectations of other more industrialised countries adopting socialism were still high, a number of developmental theorists saw the way forwards through international trade. This school of thought, which included the economist Nikolai Kondratiev, believed that the most rational path to the country's industrial development lay in Russia's trading capacity as part of the world economy. It was a strategy reminiscent of pre-revolutionary times, based on the principle of *comparative advantage*. The country's vast natural resources, including its agricultural produce, were to be exported so providing the necessary earning power to import those industrial products required for industrialisation. It was, however, a highly controversial proposal. In advocating Russia's economic dependency on a capitalist-dominated world economy, the vast majority of Bolsheviks believed that the country would be left economically and militarily vulnerable. For most of the political leadership, it was imperative to ensure that Russia's industrialisation proceeded autonomously from a world which posed a political and possibly a military threat to the establishment of a socialist country. Autonomous industrialisation, then, implied strength and a necessary power base upon which to secure the foundations for building socialism.

The industrialisation debate therefore focused on how the Soviet Union's space-economy could best be structured in order to generate the means for industrialisation and economic growth. Given the pre-eminence of the countryside in economic and social life, this necessarily involved the issue of what role the countryside's natural and human resources were to play in urban-industrial development. Two such views had emerged by the mid-1920s.

### Bukharin and balanced development

Nikolai Bukharin was one of the main supporters of Lenin's so-called New Economic Policy (NEP) which had been introduced in 1921 and which was to form the framework for development until its abrupt end in 1928–29. NEP was introduced primarily as a pragmatic measure to ensure that the countryside provided the necessary food supplies upon which the success of the Revolution depended. In essence, NEP was based on a form of territorial organisation in which a unique relationship was struck between town and countryside. On the one hand, agriculture was organised along the lines of private ownership with each of its 20 million peasant households producing what they liked both for private consumption and for sale to the towns at favourable prices. State interference in the countryside was therefore kept to a minimum. On the other hand, a large sector of the as yet small urban-industrial economy came under state (or public) ownership and control. Most notably, this included what Lenin referred to as 'the commanding heights of the economy', that is, heavy industry, the banking system, and foreign trade. For Bukharin and those who shared his organic view of the relationship between town and countryside, the mixed economy of NEP was to be based on balanced development between urban and rural areas, and would lead to slow but steady industrial growth.

The means by which industrial growth was to be achieved was through a more productive countryside. This entailed creating a favourable atmosphere for peasant agriculture in which the countryside would receive state investment comparable to that of city industry. The wealth generated from this resulting rural prosperity would enable the creation of a rural surplus which would contribute to industrial development. In addition, rural taxation would provide a supplementary source for industrial capital, but Bukharin warned that if too heavy a tax burden was imposed on the countryside, then this would lead to a lowering of agricultural production as peasant households would have less capital to reinvest and to modernise their farms. Yet while Bukharin had considerable faith in the contribution that the countryside could make to a successful industrial economy, he was far from sanguine about the question of the efficiency and reliability of private small-scale farming. The only way levels of productivity could be raised effectively, he concluded, was by encouraging the peasantry to form rural cooperatives. Such a form of social organisation can be defined as an economic association of persons of limited means, for their mutual advantage and protection. As large-scale farming units, there was considerable advantage in terms of economies of scale from peasants cooperating in this way. The rural prosperity that cooperatives would generate, Bukharin argued, would mean that the countryside would be able to purchase more industrial goods, so stimulating further industrial expansion. In addition, the setting up of rural cooperatives would be one important stage in the eventual full collectivisation of the countryside.

Alternative views on development: Nikolai Bukharin (*left*) and Evgenii Preobrazhensky.

Bukharin's optimism was however not borne out by the economic geography of the 1920s. Although the marketed output of agricultural production had recovered its pre-revolutionary level by 1927, it was insufficient to match the demographic demands of a country with six million more mouths to feed. Considerable doubt existed in the cities over the commitment of the peasantry to the NEP economy. Much of this mistrust was based on two things. Firstly, there were reports that the more enterprising peasants stored grain in order to create an urban shortage, thereby enabling the peasant to obtain a better price for grain the following year. Although no doubt this practice did occur, it is more likely that the peasantry were simply unable to meet the growing urban demand; throughout the decade periodic famines made it difficult for the countryside to feed itself, let alone meet a growing urban population. Secondly, support in the countryside for joining cooperatives met with little success. This was in spite of financial backing from the state. There were of course good reasons for apathy. In particular, and as borne out by more recent third world experience, rural attitudes and values are often contrary to external pressures for organisational or technological change; certain traditional farming practices, in spite of their inefficiency, had become an established way of life for successive generations of Russian peasants.

NEP was also characterised by negligible industrial growth with little evidence to suggest that the Bukharinist strategy would have succeeded in providing any further impetus for economic development. Without any substantive industrial progress, the urban workforce, which formed the mainstay of support for building socialism, continued to make up the same small fraction of the total population that it had in 1913: one-fifth. For many Bolsheviks, it seemed that there was little prospect of NEP providing economic stimulus to the cities. Nor without a thoroughly reorganised and mechanised rural economy would there be a 'surplus' population willing to provide the necessary additional urban labour for industrialisation.

### Preobrazhensky and differential development

Bukharin's developmental strategy put considerable faith in the countryside in delivering the necessary resources for moderate industrial growth. It was also a model which envisaged slow urban growth and only gradual change to the territorial organisation of society. For his opponents, it was a programme which naively expected that industrialisation could be financed on a shoestring budget. An alternative strategy was proposed by the economist, Evgenii Preobrazhensky. He argued that the only way to achieve industrialisation was to abandon NEP and to replace it with a fully planned space economy in which industry and the city would receive the utmost priority. In drawing upon Marx's theory of *primitive socialist accumulation*, Preobrazhensky argued that in order to ensure accelerated urban-industrial development, the government had first to exploit the resources of the non-socialist countryside. This was to involve the state underpaying the countryside for its agricultural produce and overcharging it for urban industrial goods. Savings would therefore be extracted from the countryside and hence the necessary surplus for industrial investment would be acquired. The inspiration for such a solution was drawn from that of the British Empire which in exploiting the natural resources of its colonies was able to achieve industrial growth at home. Thus the countryside was to be treated as an 'internal colony', justified on the basis of economic necessity (where else were the 'resources' for industrialisation to come from?) and on the grounds that it was the only major sector still outside state ('socialist') control, and so was contrary to the building of socialism.

This 'internal colonialism' thesis is represented in diagrammatic form in Fig. 2.2, and shows what Preobrazhensky had in mind. Surplus capital was to flow into and be invested in city industry, with the lion's share going into heavy industry. The large demand for labour which such extensive industrialisation would require, was to be met through surplus rural labour which a more mechanised and collectivised agriculture would no longer need.

Although in the short term the burden for financing industrialisation was to rest with the countryside, Preobrazhensky foresaw that in the long term, the countryside would benefit from industrialisation. Rural living standards would therefore improve and eventually match those of the city. In short, combined and uneven development would lead to more balanced development. This was for two reasons. Firstly, as a result of central planning and increased urban labour productivity, both industrial and urban consumer goods would be made available at cheaper prices to the countryside. Secondly, there would be the material and social benefits which would accrue to the peasantry from opting to join large-scale and more productive collective farms. Through their greater productivity, these farms in turn would serve as an important means of providing more capital for industrial growth and for both urban and rural housing and services.

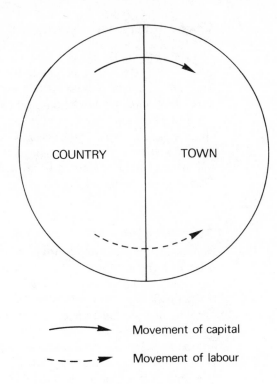

Fig. 2.2 Town-country development model: the standard 'internal colonial' view.

COUNTRY     TOWN

————▶   Movement of capital

- - - -▶   Movement of labour

## The case for rapid industrialisation

By the late 1920s, events both at home and abroad pointed increasingly
to the necessity of selecting the path to rapid industrial development.
There were a number of reasons for this. Firstly, there was the
changing international situation to consider. It seemed increasingly
apparent to the political leadership that the need for industrialisation
was caught up with the country's defensive interests and with being
militarily strong. Stalin summarised this view: 'In order to achieve the
final victory of socialism in our country, it is necessary to catch up and
surpass the advanced countries in both a technical and economic
respect. Either we achieve this or they will destroy us' (quoted in
Davies, 1978:44). Like the Empire that preceded it, the Soviet
government was only too well aware of how geographically vulnerable
Russia was to external aggressors, and how difficult it was to defend its
extensive borders in Europe, South-West Asia, Southern Asia, and on
the Pacific seaboard. Secondly, amongst the urban-based and largely
town-born political leadership, there was considerable mistrust of the
peasantry. The experiences of NEP had shown that the countryside had
little sympathy for industrialisation or socialism. It seemed neither
prepared to adopt new forms of agricultural organisation nor, if left to
its own devices, able to provide the necessary wealth for industrial
development. Finally, the political leadership was only too well aware
that without substantial economic progress, the urban population
would become increasingly disillusioned with a regime which so far had
fallen well short of its promise of improving their quality of life.

## Combined and uneven development

In most respects the developmental strategy adopted can be considered as a variant of 'internal colonialism' but is better known as the Stalinist model for development. Introduced by Joseph Stalin after the consolidation of his power base by the late 1920s, it was to effect the wholesale restructuring of Soviet society, and to place the country on a specific path to rapid and uneven development. There are three characteristics to this model which are central to its understanding and uniqueness: (1) the forced collectivisation of the countryside, (2) central planning and rapid industrialisation, and (3) mass migration.

### Forced collectivisation

The most significant departure from the two developmental models described above concerns the means by which collectivisation was to be achieved. All agreed that collectivisation was essential to constructing a socialist society, but where the ideas of Bukharin and Preobrazhensky depart from the Stalinist model is that they saw it as a voluntary process. For Stalin, neither the timescale nor the practices and performance of the peasant economy lent themselves to such evolutionism. Draconian methods and techniques therefore became the first and most important hallmark of collectivisation in the 1929–32 period. By 1937, 93 percent of peasant households had been collectivised compared with only 1.7 percent in 1928 (*Nar. Khoz. SSSR v 1958g.*: 346). Collectivisation and the establishment of the collective farm (*kolkhoz*) as the main form of rural organisation was to result in the full integration of the countryside into a centrally planned economy. This meant that the state could determine what the countryside should produce and in what quantity. By establishing a near monopoly over the purchase of agricultural produce, it could also fix the prices to be paid for commodities. The state thus had complete control over 'the terms of trade' with the countryside. The amount of produce demanded by the state was fixed at a high level and the price it paid to the collectives was low. On this basis, the surplus generated as a result of collectivisation was to finance industrialisation.

### Central planning and rapid industrialisation

The drive towards rapid industrialisation was launched with the adoption of the first Five Year Plan (FYP) in 1928. Its pattern of capital investment bears a close resemblance to Preobrazhensky's industrialisation programme; between 1928 and 1936 investment was biased towards industry, with agriculture and other sectors of the economy and social welfare receiving a smaller share, particularly by 1936 (Table 2.2). Differentials were even more marked if we compare economic growth in the industrial sector with that in the agricultural sector; agricultural production grew at an annual rate of only 1 percent between 1928 and 1937, whereas industrial production grew at an annual rate of 11 percent. But such uneven development was not confined to differences between town and country; within the towns there was a definite pro-heavy industry bias (towards, for example, iron and steel, machine building, coal, and defence-related industries).

**Table 2.2   Investment in fixed capital, 1928 and 1936***

| | 1928 | 1936 | 1936 index |
| --- | --- | --- | --- |
| | (thousand million rubles) | | (1928 = 100) |
| Gross investment in fixed capital, | 6.34 | 39.60 | 625 |
| of which | | | |
|    industry | 1.81 | 14.90 | 823 |
|    agriculture | 1.40 | >3.40 | >243 |
|    transport and communications | 0.90 | 6.84 | 728 |
|    education and health | 0.23 | 0.98 | 426 |
|    housing (urban and rural) | 1.71 | 2.14 | 125 |

* based on soviet data at current prices.
*Source:* S. G. Wheatcroft *et al.* (1986) 'Soviet industrialisation reconsidered: some preliminary conclusions about economic development between 1926 and 1941', *Economic History Review* 39(2), p. 275.

Between 1928 and 1937, heavy manufacturing industry's net product share of total manufacturing more than doubled, from 31 to 63 percent, whereas light manufacturing's product share fell from 68 to 36 percent (Gregory and Stuart, 1986: 34). Savings on urban infrastructural facilities (housing, transport, fuel and power supplies) along with state-fixed low urban wages also helped to finance heavy industry.

The priority afforded to heavy industry did not radically alter the geography of capital investment during the 1930s. Capital investment projects and new factory development tended to be located in and around those industrial conurbations which had been the main focus of activity during the late nineteenth century, namely Moscow, Leningrad (St Petersburg), and the Donbass. Better developed infrastructural facilities in combination with a plentiful supply of labour for a planned economy concerned with maximising short-term returns on investment determined such a pattern. European USSR therefore accounted for a larger proportion of Soviet industrial output in 1940 than it did in 1926. Yet the industrialisation drive did mark a new phase in the economic development of the Eastlands. From the second FYP (1933–37) onwards, a number of large-scale capital investment projects were established, associated particularly with the additional energy resources and raw materials required by rapidly industrialising European USSR, which Siberia possessed in abundance.

The uneven impact of planned development in the cities of European USSR was also to have a profound and lasting effect. The channelling of a disproportionately large amount of capital into developing the heavy industrial economy of particularly the largest and oldest cities went hand in hand with the demand for a large labour force. City authorities could not begin to cope with the demands made by industry for a new labour force which in the wake of forced collectivisation was flooding into urban areas. Newly arrived rural migrants were forced either to share one-apartment rooms in unbelievably overcrowded conditions or to live in hurriedly constructed shacks. The outcome of the demand for city labour exceeding the availability of housing is known as *underurbanisation*. Its long-term impact will be considered in the next chapter. In order to cope with this situation, the state's response was to impose restrictions on the further demographic and industrial expansion of Moscow and Leningrad in 1931. However, the interests of extensive industrialisation and its need for a large labour force in order to ensure high levels of industrial output, dictated otherwise.

## Mass rural-to-urban migration

As in most societies, economic growth is a major stimulant to population redistribution. Where the Soviet developmental experience of the 1930s differs from other societies undergoing parallel changes in rural-to-urban and in inter-regional migrations, is in the sheer scale and intensity of its demographic redistribution. It also differs in that it was not simply the more usual case of industrialisation 'pulling' labour from the countryside but also of collectivisation 'pushing' labour out of agriculture. In short, Stalinist development produced a demographic upheaval on such a scale that by the late 1930s few people were where they had been a decade earlier.

In the 1926–39 intercensal period, the city population more or less doubled, from 26.3 million to 56.1 million. The urban share of the total USSR population increased from 17.9 percent to 32.8 percent. Most of this urban growth occurred west of the Urals, particularly in the Moscow and Leningrad regions, and in the Ukraine (Fig. 2.3). At least two-fifths of this urban growth was due to net migration. Between 1928 and 1938, annual net migration into the country's cities only fell once below the one million mark (in 1933), reaching a height in 1931 when on balance the cities gained 4.1 million workers from the countryside (Lorimer, 1946:150).

Fig. 2.3 Urban growth in the USSR, 1926–39.

It is unlikely that such a scale of rural outmigration over this short period would have been possible without forced collectivisation. Mass

26

starvation and exceptional rural hardship, in combination with opposition to joining collective farms, provided industrialisation with a plentiful supply of labour. With the notable exception of the Moscow district, where the rural population actually increased, declines in the rural population were characteristic. Besides migration this was also due to high rural mortality caused by famine and 'the terror'. Nowhere was rural depopulation so marked as in the rich and fertile steppe stretching from the southern Ukraine to Kazakhstan. It was in this region that collectivisation was most extensive and where agriculture was the most mechanised. The population from this region that survived to become surplus to the requirements of collectivisation found its way into the towns and cities. In all, the rural population of Kazakhstan declined by one-fifth and of the Ukraine by a sixth.

According to the internal colonialism model (see Fig. 2.2), the rural economy functioned as a contributor to the development process by supplying capital and labour resources to the urban-industrial economy. Yet doubts have recently been raised about the actual contribution of collectivisation to industrialisation. More recent evidence from a period notoriously difficult to reconstruct owing to limited data, challenges two particular aspects of what had become the standard story of events:

1   Whether the countryside was actually neglected by state investment to the extent that what was 'saved' contributed to urban-industrial development.
2   The extent to which collectivisation was necessary in order to provide the large volume of labour for extensive industrialisation in the cities.

## The countryside's contribution to industrialisation

The evidence challenging the view that the countryside was necessarily neglected comes from the Soviet economist, A. A. Barsov (1969). He not only questions whether savings were exacted from the countryside in order to provide for industrialisation, but goes further in suggesting that in the crucial first FYP period, the countryside was actually a net recipient of state capital. The 'internal colonialism thesis' of urban-industrial bias is therefore turned on its head. According to Barsov, there was a net flow of state resources into three particular sectors of the rural economy: the machine tractor stations, state farms, and the private plot (Fig. 2.4).

### Machine tractor stations (MTS)

Although initially set up in 1927, the MTS were expanded primarily in order to provide the machinery to collective farms that had few resources, in the wake of the massive destruction of capital stock (e.g. draught animals) following forced collectivisation. The MTS did however provide another important function: given the lack of loyal party members in the rural areas and the mistrust of the authorities towards the collectives, the MTS were a way in which the state could keep an eye on developments in the countryside. Each MTS would rent

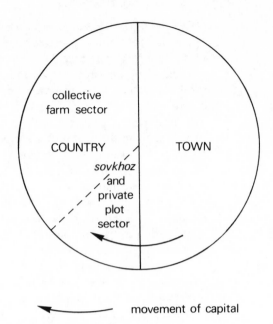

collective
farm sector

COUNTRY          TOWN

sovkhoz
and
private
plot
sector

Fig. 2.4 Town-country
development model: Barsov's
interpretation.

←————————  movement of capital

to collective farms within its local jurisdiction, machinery for ploughing, harvesting or haulage. For the state, it was a way of providing scarce machinery which collectives could not afford to purchase out of meagre budgets. According to Barsov, as a result of expanding the MTS, the amount of machinery made available by the state to the countryside increased 2.2 times between 1928 and 1932. While one should not doubt the important economic function of the MTS, it is vital to remind ourselves that there were a number of obstacles to them contributing to increased production on the collectives. Firstly, the excessively high state-fixed rental charges for machinery were often way beyond what the average collective could afford. Secondly, given the seasonal demand for particular types of machinery, the MTS was often unable to meet the requirements of all collective farms in its area. Consequently, having to rely on the often inadequate services of the MTS, the production schedules of the farms were unduly affected.

### State farms (or *sovkhozy*)

Unlike collective farms, state or *sovkhoz* farms are directly financed by the state. All their 'inputs', including machinery, fertilisers and the like, come directly out of state coffers. Moreover, in contrast to the collective farms whose employees are dependent for wages on the often limited profits that accrue from their collective, state farm workers, because they are classified as 'workers' and not as 'peasants', receive a fixed 'state' wage like their urban counterparts. Consequently, *sovkhoz* workers were usually much better off than collective farm workers. There was therefore a considerable flow of resources going into this rural sector. But although generally larger and more productive than the average collective, during the 1930s the state farm sector was of minor significance in comparison with the collectives. State farms probably totalled no more than 4,000 by 1940 compared with 237,000 collectives (*Nar. Khoz. SSSR v 1984g.*:223).

### The private plot

Finally, Barsov identifies the private plot as an important net recipient of resources. The peasantry, having to endure the trauma of collectivisation, were granted one major concession: each peasant household could retain a small plot of land. After daily commitments to the collective were completed, the household was free to farm its private plot. Besides providing a necessary means of subsistence for the family, the peasant was permitted to sell what he produced from the plot on the open market, thereby providing the household with a vital source of additional income. This arrangement well-suited the state, faced as it was with the chronic urban shortages of food, particularly of market-gardening-type produce. As a result, through the private market the private plot provided for more than half of all potatoes consumed, 18 percent of other vegetables, 61 percent of milk, and 55 percent of meat (*Nar. Khoz. SSSR v 1970g.*:283). Barsov therefore argues that as a consequence of the low state prices paid to the collective to meet the costs of investment in heavy industry, this had the effect of ensuring higher prices for produce sold on the open market to urban consumers. The urban population, he concludes, made a far greater sacrifice.

Much of Barsov's claims about the amount of resources going into the countryside rests on his choice of 1926–27 as the baseline to calculate prices, but the pros and cons of this argument need not detain us. What is important is that Barsov is claiming that in the first FYP period, there was a net flow of resources not into all sectors of the rural economy but into particular sectors. In other words, gains were specific, with the state sector (state farms) and the private plot benefiting while the collective farms benefited indirectly from the MTS.

There is no doubt that the urban labour force sacrificed much for industrial growth. Urban wages were kept purposely low in order to channel scarce resources into industrialisation. We have also noted that the state spent far less on housing the urban worker or providing other much-needed amenities and services. But there is no concrete evidence to suggest that urban workers suffered more than the peasantry. Table 2.3 illustrates this. It presents data on food consumption per capita of the rural and urban population for the crucial years 1928 and 1932.

**Table 2.3  Food consumption in town and countryside, 1928 and 1932**

|  | Bread and grains | Potatoes | Meat |
|---|---|---|---|
|  | | kg per caput | |
| Town | | | |
| 1928 | 174.4 | 87.6 | 51.7 |
| 1932 | 211.3 | 110.0 | 16.9 |
| Countryside | | | |
| 1928 | 250.4 | 141.1 | 24.8 |
| 1932 | 214.6 | 125.0 | 11.2 |

*Source:* J. Millar and A. Nove (1976) 'A debate on Soviet collectivisation. Was Stalin really necessary?' *Problems of Communism*, July/August.

It shows that in 1928, the countryside was marginally better off than the towns, although rural inhabitants had less of a meat-based diet. By 1932, however, with the sharp fall in the quality of food available to the cities, the urban population was forced to fill themselves up with potatoes and bread. But we can also see that by that year, the countryside ate less of everything. These figures would therefore suggest that the burden of industrial change was not borne primarily by either the urban or the rural population but by both.

## The contribution of the GULag labour force

The other debate centres on the question of whether collectivisation was necessary in order to provide the large volume of labour required by the cities for industrialisation. There is no doubt that by the late 1920s, there were probably as many as three million people unemployed in the cities, in part a consequence of the slow industrial growth strategy of NEP. But given the scale of subsequent industrialisation, it is very unlikely, even with this 'urban surplus', that the requirements of the rapidly expanding urban-industrial sector could have been met. The countryside's reorganisation was necessary, for it is doubtful whether without forced collectivisation the rural population would have voluntarily moved into the cities. What this debate has raised, however, is the previously neglected contribution that the 1930s penal labour force made to industrialisation.

In addition to mass rural-urban migration, there was a second major migration stream which emerged during the 1930s: the forced movement of both rural and urban populations into the work camps in the so-called 'GULag Archipelago' of Siberia and the Northlands. It is impossible to ascertain exactly how many 'enemies of the state' were incarcerated by the late 1930s. In 1928, there were probably no more than 30,000 inmates. It has been estimated that if we include both those who were incarcerated in the camps and those who were employed in their administration, then by 1940 its population was around 10 million (Rosefielde, 1980). Most certainly, however, its membership was drawn from both town and country, although in the 1929–32 period, the principal source was the latter, with the richer peasants (*kulaks*, that group singled out by Stalin as being 'anti-socialist' and as responsible for 'hoarding grain') making up the largest proportion. In all, at the height of collectivisation, the rural population made up between 70 and 80 percent of the labour camps' 3.5 million workforce. By the late 1930s, however, the city was also supplying the camps with labour. In short, all walks of life – urban and rural, peasant and urban worker, party and non-party members – were affected, for no individual, social grouping or geographical community was immune from Stalin's 'terror'.

Up until recently it was thought that on balance and in spite of an undoubtedly large labour force, the labour camp contribution to overall national development must have been minimal. The following case, involving the building of the Belomor Canal, is typical of the image held of an incompetent GULag sector contributing little to industrialisation. In the early 1930s, the decision was taken to build a canal linking Leningrad to the White Sea port of Kem (Fig. 2.5). The logic behind the scheme appears to have been weak; there was already

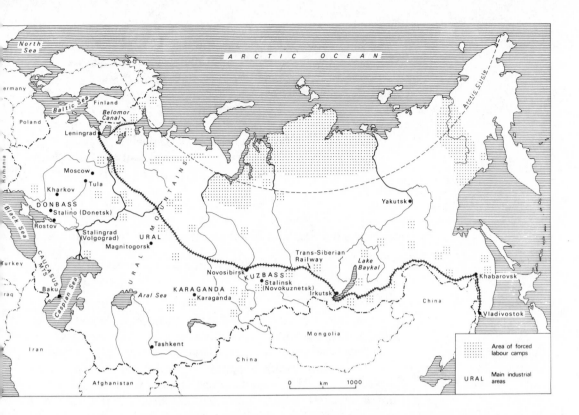

Figure labels on map: North Sea; ARCTIC OCEAN; Germany; Poland; Baltic Sea; Finland; Belomor Canal; Leningrad; Moscow; Tula; Kharkov; Rumania; Black Sea; DONBASS; Stalino (Donetsk); Rostov; Stalingrad (Volgograd); URAL; Magnitogorsk; Turkey; CAUCASUS MTS; Baku; Caspian Sea; Iraq; Aral Sea; KARAGANDA; Karaganda; Novosibirsk; KUZBASS; Stalinsk (Novokuznetsk); Trans-Siberian Railway; Lake Baykal; Irkutsk; Yakutsk; Khabarovsk; China; Vladivostok; Mongolia; Tashkent; China; Iran; Afghanistan; Arctic Circle; URAL MOUNTAINS

Legend: Area of forced labour camps; URAL Main industrial areas

0 km 1000

Fig. 2.5 Regional development under Stalin.

a rail network and there was no obvious strategic advantage in providing an alternative mode of communication. From 1931 until 1933, over 200,000 prisoners laboured in the most extreme climatic and environmental conditions using the technology of the Stone Age to meet Stalin's production schedule. Casualties were phenomenally high. Yet the canal was opened on time, despite the fact that its dykes were made of earth and its floodgates of wood. It was however of little use; its main channel was only 5 metres deep, which precluded ocean-going vessels.

Yet the contribution of the GULag economy should not be underestimated. We know, for instance, that the use of slave labour kept costs low and that certainly by the second five year plan (1933–37), the sheer number of inmates, even if their labour was not optimally used, must have been of significance to economic growth. Even by 1933, the penal labour force made up as much as a third of the total non-agrarian labour force in industry and construction. Yet despite the incarceration of specialist labour, it was not deployed that efficiently; using civil engineers or physicists to dig canals could hardly have been economically beneficial. We also know that petty officials responsible for the administration of these camps exaggerated their contribution in an attempt to convince central planners of fulfilment of their production plan. So widespread was this practice that a name was invented for it: *tukhta*, meaning 'padding of worksheets'. This practice, however, was not confined to the camps; it was also to be found in other sectors of the urban-industrial economy. So universal was the practice, it is probable that official Soviet estimates of overall economic performance were also on the high side. What this may mean then is that the contribution of the non-GULag urban-industrial sector may

31

not be as high as previously thought and that the contribution of the GULag labour force might be significant.

Without doubt, however, GULag labour made a significant contribution to the regional transformation of Siberia and the Northlands (Fig. 2.5). For instance, penal labour was used in the construction of such cities as Sovetskaya Gavan, Magadan, Norilsk, Vorkuta and Nakhodka. It was also partly responsible for the development of both the Kuznetsk and Magnitogorsk industrial complexes, for the building of numerous canals, railways, and hydro-electric power stations, and later, in the setting up of the country's first nuclear power plants.

### Reassessing the Stalinist developmental model

The Stalinist model for development possesses a number of characteristics which distinguish it from non-socialist countries undergoing economic development.

1  The goal-oriented and planned nature of the development process distinguishes the Soviet experience from that of non-socialist countries. The Soviet state possesses a powerful facility in its ownership of the means of production and it was this which made it possible for planning preferences, as determined by political decision-makers, to single out particular sectors of the economy for special treatment. To this end, the Soviet developmental experience can be judged successful in that its broad aims of achieving industrialisation and collectivisation were realised.

2  The magnitude and speed of industrialisation which occurred in the Soviet Union during the 1930s has no parallel in non-socialist countries undergoing industrial development or for that matter in any other socialist country. Many Western countries have yet to attain a heavy industry share of manufacturing as large as the USSR's in 1939. The scale of migration and rate of urbanisation which also occurred during this period required from fifty to seventy-five years in other countries.

3  Usually a country's dependence on foreign trade is gradually reduced in the course of development. In the Soviet case, this was particularly so. The ratio of exports to national income declined dramatically, from 3.5 percent in 1930 to 0.5 percent in 1937. Such a near-withdrawal from the world economy was mainly due to its forced isolation from contact with the rest of the world on a scale not paralleled by any other non-socialist country and matched by few of today's socialist states (Kampuchea in the 1975–78 period and Albania up until very recently are probable exceptions).

4  Few countries in the throes of development avoid the human suffering and misery associated with industrialisation and rapid urban growth. Indeed, it was precisely the social deprivation and misery that Britain's industrial revolution produced which provided much of the inspiration for the writings of Marx and Engels. No country, however, matches the extent to which development was achieved in the USSR at the expense of its population.

*Summary*

The 1930s experience of combined and uneven development, bequeathed to subsequent generations, has been a legacy which has endured the test of time. And yet, since the mid-1950s, successive Soviet leaders have attempted to alter the basic fabric of its geography through, for instance, allocating more capital investment to the countryside and to programmes of social spending. There have also been successive attempts to reform the overly centralised planning and political decision-making process but these have been invariably defeated by those institutions – like the industrial ministries – which still owe their power to the economic priorities set out in the 1930s. It is with this Stalinist legacy of combined and uneven development in mind that the task of the reform-minded leader, Gorbachev, to restructure the Soviet economy, has to be understood.

# 3  Underurbanisation, social inequality and city development

The course of urbanisation in the Soviet Union differs from that observed in non-socialist countries. In the developed countries of Western Europe and North America, the state did little to regulate the flow of rural and small-town migrants into the cities. Similarly , in the developing world, Latin American and Afro-Asian governments have not been able to prevent the mass influx of migrants who have abandoned their villages for cities. Such poor capitalist countries suffer from what has been labelled *overurbanisation*. In essence it means that there is more labour than urban employment and housing. A consequence of this mismatch is the growth of the shanty-town, an only too familiar feature of the hardship and deprivation of third world cities. In contrast, the Soviet Union has tried to control the process of urbanisation during most of its seventy-year history by attempting to regulate the demographic growth of its major cities. Such a policy has been partly motivated by the necessity of having to cope with urban housing shortages and overburdened city services. Moreover, in stark contrast to the third world experience, the demand for urban labour exceeds its supply. This largely unintended imbalance between the greater availability of urban jobs than places to live in the city can be called *underurbanisation*. In this chapter we examine this phenomenon and the social and economic consequences it has for the territorial organisation of urban life.

## Urban growth and city development

Few countries match the sheer speed at which the Soviet Union has been transformed into an urbanised society. On the eve of Stalin's industrialisation programme, 26.3 percent of the population were living in cities. Only a decade later, this had increased to 39.5 percent. Urban growth in the post-war years has continued at a rapid pace, with the urban population increasing its relative share of the total population from 47.9 percent (100 million) in 1959 to 66.2 percent (187.5 million) by 1987. The Soviet Union is now only second to the United States in the total number of people living in urban areas.

This growth, however, has been highly uneven, with the larger cities, both initially and into modern times, growing at a faster pace than medium-sized towns (50,000–100,000 inhabitants) and small towns (those under 50,000 inhabitants). In the most recent intercensal period (1970–79), the urban share of the population of cities between 50,000 and 250,000 persons actually declined. At the same time, the share of cities with populations of over 250,000 in relation to the total number of urban inhabitants increased from 46.6 percent in 1970 to over 50 percent by 1979. An even more significant increase is detectable in the share of the urban population living in so-called 'millionaire' cities.

The demographic growth of these large cities has led to a whole variety of socio-economic problems. It has exacerbated the housing shortage and led to overcrowding and to a phenomenal increase in daily commuting as workers are pushed into the suburbs in order to find accommodation. The heavily utilised urban public transport system is consequently stretched to its limits. With increasing pressure on the city to invest in the brick and mortar of large-scale house-building programmes, the surrounding green belt and good farming land comes under threat. City authorities which are responsible for providing a range of consumer services out of their limited city budgets find it difficult to meet this increasing demographic demand. As Sigov (1986:46) admits,

Analysis of the fulfilment of the master plans of a number of the country's largest cities and megalopolises shows that many of them have significantly exceeded the population ceiling in accordance with which plans for the development of their urban infrastructure were developed. This results in certain disproportion between the size of the population and existing facilities in the service sphere.

As might be expected given its urban primacy and inordinate appeal as a place to live and work, this situation is especially problematic in the country's largest city. According to Bialkovskaya and Novikov (1982:89), this has led to 'the level of satisfaction of Moscow's population requirements for various services to be only 50–60 percent of the level specified in the master plan of its development [in the area of housing and municipal services].'

How then are we to explain this uneven demographic growth which is evidently recognised by policymakers and urban specialists as leading to such problems for the large city and its inhabitants? We do not get much explanatory mileage by focusing on the natural population increase (the excess of births over deaths) of large cities. As Table 3.1 shows, for most millionaire and major cities (those grouped into Types 1 and 2), natural population increase is less significant in accounting for the cities' demographic reproduction than is gain through net migration. In *Type 1* cities in particular, all of which are located in European USSR, natural population growth has been falling quite

**Table 3.1 A typology of population reproduction for the USSR's millionaire and major cities**

| Type | Characteristics | Number of cities | Cities |
|------|-----------------|------------------|--------|
| 1 | NMI > NPI | 11 | Moscow, Leningrad, Riga, Odessa, Kharkov, Gorkii, Dnepropetrovsk, Tallinn, Kiev, Vilnius, Kishinev |
| 2 | NMI = NPI | 8 | Alma-Ata, Donetsk, Sverdlovsk, Kuybyshev, Novosibirsk, Minsk, Tashkent, Kazan |
| 3 | NMI < NPI | 7 | Tbilisi, Chelyabinsk, Frunze, Omsk, Ashkhabad, Yerevan, Baku |

NMI = net migration increase
NPI = natural population increase
*Source:* V. Bialkovskaya and V. Novikov (1982) 'Urbanizatsiya i problemy organicheniya rosta krupneishikh gorodov', *Voprosy Ekonomiki* 11, p. 93.

dramatically since the early 1960s. In Moscow, for example, it has fallen from 6.9 per thousand population to 1.4 per thousand by the 1980s. This is primarily due to a falling birth rate associated with changing social attitudes linked to modern urban life styles, but is also a consequence of the general ageing of the population resulting from the improved quality of city life. In contrast, urban growth in *Type 3* cities is still largely due to persistently high birth rates linked in Muslim Central Asia in particular to the desirability of a large family. Moreover, unlike most large cities in European USSR where migration has now reached the stage of being overwhelmingly inter-urban, in *Type 3* cities migration remains a predominantly rural-to-urban phenomenon. This is again especially the case in Muslim Central Asia.

But given that most millionaire cities are located in European USSR, we can generalise by saying that it is migration which accounts for most large-city demographic growth. Large cities may however be growing at a faster pace than other towns and they may also constitute the largest proportion of urban residents, but compared with most other industrialised countries, the Soviet Union *still* has far fewer of its urban population living in large cities. Rowland (1983) estimates that the USSR's share of millionaire cities measured as a proportion of its urban population stands at 15 percent compared with the worldwide average of 32 percent. More specifically, as Table 3.2 illustrates, if we compare the USSR and those socialist countries at a similar level of development with a number of non-socialist countries which to varying degrees are roughly comparable to the USSR's developmental stage, then typically the proportion of the urban population living in large cities in the socialist world is smaller.

And so we have a seeming paradox to the urbanisation process in the Soviet Union: *Large cities continue to grow at a faster pace than*

**Table 3.2  Percentage of the urban population of selected countries living in cities of over 500,000 persons**

|  | 1960 | 1980 |
|---|---|---|
| *Socialist countries* | | |
| Soviet Union | 21 | 33 |
| Czechoslovakia | 17 | 12 |
| German Democratic Republic | 14 | 17 |
| Hungary | 45 | 37 |
| *Industrialised market economies* | | |
| United States of America | 61 | 77 |
| German Federal Republic | 48 | 45 |
| Japan | 35 | 42 |
| Sweden | 15 | 35 |
| United Kingdom | 66 | 55 |
| *Most industrialised of the third world market economies* | | |
| Argentina | 54 | 60 |
| Brazil | 35 | 52 |
| Mexico | 36 | 48 |
| South Korea | 61 | 70 |

*Source:* World Bank, *World Development Report 1987*, Oxford University Press, Oxford, pp. 266–7.

*other towns and yet compared with most parts of the industrialised world, there are fewer urban inhabitants living in large cities.* So on the one hand it would seem that there are important urban processes working for the growth of large cities in relation to other towns and yet on the other hand uniquely Soviet constraints have had an impact on limiting the proportion of urban inhabitants living in large cities. Let us then explore both aspects of this apparent paradox; first, the reasons for the unevenness in city growth, and second, the constraints on the demographic development of large cities.

## Differential urban development

In keeping with the aim of industrial and demographic deconcentration, the state has pursued a policy of containing new industrial development in large cities. In 1931 construction of new industries in Moscow and Leningrad was prohibited. Eight years later this prohibition was extended to include five more cities (Kiev, Kharkov, Rostov, Gorkii and Sverdlovsk). In the post-war years, this policy has been expanded to include more or less all cities with populations of more than 500,000, together with many other large towns. According to recent pronouncements, this scheme will continue to form a cornerstone of industrial location policy. Guidelines for the country's social and economic development to the year 2000 call for a restriction on the creation of new industrial enterprises in large cities, with the exception of personal service facilities, and for the continuing encouragement of the formation and expansion of enterprises in small and medium-sized towns. Laudable as these aims may be, they have not halted the industrial and demographic expansion of large cities. According to Rowland's (1983) calculations, the forty-seven cities earmarked for no more new industrial concentration in 1956 recorded a demographic increase of 2.2 percent between 1959 and 1979 compared with only a slightly higher city-wide national average of 2.5 percent.

The main reason why large city growth continues in spite of attempts by city and national planners to plan for the contrary is to do with the power and importance of industrial interests in Soviet society. The dominance of these interests in facilitating urbanisation stems from the continuing significance that the state places on securing high national returns from industrial growth, with the result that the industrial ministries play a leading role in urbanisation and in the social life of the city. Large cities have much to offer industry. As a number of Soviet writers have shown, due to economies of scale there is a tendency for economic productivity of industry to increase with the size of a city. This stems from the more developed physical infrastructure (most notably, transport), the concentration and availability of skilled labour, and readily accessible markets of the larger urban areas. In a country so geared towards fulfilling and over-fulfilling plans, it would seem logical that large cities should continue to receive investment priority from industrial ministries which themselves are constantly under pressure to increase production as rapidly as possible. What then has taken place in large cities is a self-reproducing process. The continuing expansion of industry gives further impetus to the urban economy which then fuels the demand for more labour from outside the city. This in turn necessitates the growth in employment of an over-stretched service sector in order to meet the needs of an ever-expanding city population.

There are cases where the industrial ministries openly flaunt planning decrees by locating new industry in cities designated for no new factory development. One official source notes that in the Ukraine, new industrial enterprises are being located in the region's largest cities rather than in the intended smaller and medium-sized towns (Stanislavskii, 1974:48). A more usual situation involves a number of the older cities in the European part of the country which have been designated for no new factory development. Many of their industries are old and in need of renovation. Here the intention is that 'industry develops primarily as a result of the more rational use of the existing production material and the reconstruction and technical retooling of existing enterprises without an increase in the size of the workforce' (Sigov, 1986:45). Policy stipulates that plans can only be remodelled if production can be raised at least threefold. But as a consequence of remodelling Kiev's motor industry, its workforce doubled. In another instance, also involving the ministry responsible for the automobile industry, a decision was taken to expand production at Gorkii, a city earmarked for restricted industrial development, by introducing an assembly-line plant for making cabins for trucks. The ministry responsible guaranteed that 'the interests of the city would be taken into account' (Trube, 1985). But as noted later, 'However, when the matter had progressed to the stage of expert evaluation and ratifications, expenditures for these purposes [for looking after city interests] had to a large extent been eliminated. As a result, what suffered were the interests of the workers of the autoplant itself, and the autoplant's region, where more than 300,000 persons lived' (*Gor'kovskaya Pravda*, 22 June 1984). So the automobile industry failed to take cognisance of the necessary investments required for the city's physical and social infrastructure. As a result of this decision, a larger labour force was required which could only be provided from outside the city. According to Trube (1985), behaviour such as this has led to negative consequences for Gorkii's social amenities; the availability of its theatres, cinemas, shops, restaurants and services is now only 50–80 percent of the norm for the Russian republic.

The power that the industrial ministries exert over investment allocations brings industry into conflict with other city interests. Much of this stems from a system of sectoral and territorial planning in which the former has dominated. Under sectoral planning, a given ministry (e.g. machine building, electronics, construction) is responsible for developing a given branch of the economy on a national basis. In contrast, responsibility for territorial planning lies with particular regional units, be it cities or regions. The latter, however, because of their limited power and financial muscle, find it difficult to plan for the more balanced development of their communities. Consequently, investment tends to favour those cities that the sectorally-organised industrial ministries favour.

One important consequence of the power of industrial-ministerial interests over those of the city concerns the significance to the industrial ministries of housing in making decisions about where to invest in factory development. In Soviet cities, responsibility for housing is dominated by the industrial ministries and town soviets (local government). In many cities, it is the industrial ministries which own most of the housing and which take on the responsibility for its construction and upkeep. In the Donetsk region, for example, the Ministry of Coal controls 27.9 percent of Donetsk housing, other ministries 18.2 percent and local soviets 25.8 percent (Ross, 1986:157). But ministerial concern with maximising industrial investment and utilising what capital the ministry has to its fullest productive capacity means that the building and maintenance of housing is treated as being of secondary importance because it falls into the non-productive sphere of economic activity. Consequently, large cities are attractive to industrial ministries because not only do large cities have a larger capital budget for housing but there already exists a large town soviet-maintained housing sector in these cities. From a purely short-term and pragmatic production point of view, it makes more sense for industrial ministries to invest in these cities. The alternative is to invest in smaller or new towns, many of which have only a limited housing budget and where large amounts of overhead capital would be required by an industrial ministry for housing its workers. So the smaller towns find it difficult to attract industrial funds partly because of inadequately provided town soviet housing and other social amenities and services.

It is also worth noting that where industrial ministries have invested in small towns, owing to a limited town budget they have had to take on a greater responsibility for housing and consumer services. The life of these so-called 'enterprise towns' is dominated by one or two industrial ministries. The town of Rustavi in Georgia is one example. Founded in the mid-1940s, it has two factories, a metallurgical plant and a chemical combine, which together have more or less total control over the city's development, having responsibility for housing, heating and water supply, public transportation, and many other urban services. In cities like this, the availability and standard of consumer services are likely to be poorer than in the larger cities because of the lower priority given by the industrial ministries to the non-productive sphere.

*Housing demand and variability*

Overcrowding and long waiting lists for accommodation are more or less universal phenomena of Soviet cities. Yet, compared with the past, far more attention is now paid by the state to the housing problem. This is reflected in the marked increase in capital allocated to the town soviets and by the industrial ministries for the building and maintenance of housing. As a result of a series of ambitious house-building programmes, beginning in the mid-1950s, the average living space per person (the measure used by planners as an indicator of housing quality) has increased from 8.8 square metres to the present-day figure of 13.2 square metres. There is, however, considerable variation in housing conditions for the Russian republic (Table 3.3). Both city-budgetary and industrial-sectoral methods of allocation are largely responsible for these continuing inter-urban disparities. The best accommodation, therefore, is to be found in the major cities. In smaller towns and in the new towns of Siberia and the Northlands, housing construction lags well behind industrial investment. The suburbs of large metropolitan areas (many of which would be classified as either small or medium-sized towns) often fair little better. There, cramped high-rise apartments – set as they are in urban environments which offer poor shopping and recreational facilities, unpaved and frequently muddy walks to the bus, and a long trip to work – have limited appeal as places to live.

Despite offering better housing conditions, the pressure on the major cities to embark upon more house-building is considerable. This is especially so given the social problems that the city now faces as a consequence of the demand for places to live. Soviet urban planners and sociologists have noted with growing concern the relationship between poor housing conditions and the increasing rates of alcoholism and divorce amongst the urban population.

**Table 3.3   Housing space, 1960 and 1975**

|              | 1960 | 1975 |
|--------------|------|------|
|              | m² per caput | |
| Moscow       | 9.7  | 14.8 |
| Large cities | 8.1  | 11.5 |
| Medium towns | 7.7  | 11.1 |
| Small towns  | 7.7  | 10.7 |

Keys to the flats for new tenants from the Zheleznodorozhny district of Novosibirsk.

*Source:* C. Nechemias (1981) 'The impact of Soviet housing policy on housing conditions in Soviet cities: the uneven push from Moscow', *Urban Studies* 18, p. 6.

## The role of the passport

Urban growth may be greatest in the largest cities due to the advantages of large-scale production, but how do we explain the fact that the proportion of urban dwellers in large cities is lower in Soviet and East European countries than in comparably developed market economies? Part of the answer to this rests with the role that the internal passport system plays in regulating the population's geographical mobility. Having to carry a passport in order to move around Russia is not a new phenomenon. It existed during the reign of Peter the Great (1689–1725) and, because it carries with it particular privileges for its holder, it has long since been acknowledged as a pocket reminder of position and status in society. Its pre-revolutionary social significance is neatly captured in an old tsarist adage which describes the individual as consisting of three vital elements: body, soul and passport. Fifteen years after the Revolution, in 1932, the passport was reintroduced. The pretext for this decision was that it would provide a means of regulating the flood of labour into the major cities at a time when the city authorities could not cope with the scale of in-migration triggered by forced collectivisation and the first Five Year Plan. It was therefore to take on the role of controlling the migration process. Passports were issued to urban workers as a right but were denied the bulk of the rural population, the peasantry. So in theory at least, without a passport the peasantry could not freely leave their collective farm and settle in the city.

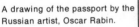
A drawing of the passport by the Russian artist, Oscar Rabin.

The passport system, however, went further than this. In the same year, residence permits or *propiski* were reintroduced. In order to obtain a *propiska* (equivalent to a visa), for which a passport was a necessary prerequisite, a migrant wishing to reside in a large city had to apply, as now, to the local city authorities. A *propiska* is typically granted only if a migrant can obtain housing and employment in the city. The non-issuance of a *propiska* has therefore become an important sanction which planners and city authorities use for large cities as a means of controlling demographic growth. These cities have been officially designated as 'closed cities' which means that they have been earmarked as places where in-migration is to be restricted or halted altogether. They have also tended to be those places singled out for no more new factory development. In the post-war years the number of closed cities has grown rapidly. As Fig. 3.1 shows, more or less all urban places with a population of over 500,000, together with a number of smaller towns, have been designated the status of 'closed city'.

There is little doubt that the use of the passport-*propiska* system to restrict the demographic growth of large cities is far from being watertight. In the early years in particular, when the success of industrialisation depended on the massive inflow of both rural and small-town labour, little effort was made to monitor whether migrants possessed the necessary documentary right to settle and work in the large city. Nowadays city authorities are less lax. Yet ways around living and working in the city without being a *propiska*-holder exist as the following two common practices illustrate.

One way involves factory managers who, in need of labour, will either turn a blind eye if a migrant does not possess the necessary

Fig. 3.1  Soviet cities subject to some form of industrial-demographic restriction.

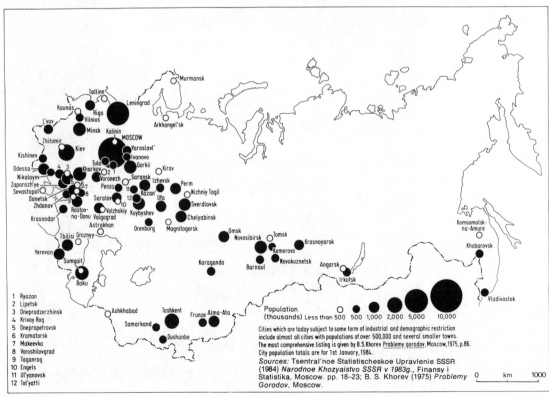

1 Ryazan
2 Lipetsk
3 Dneprodzerzhinsk
4 Krivoy Rog
5 Dnepropetrovsk
6 Kramatorsk
7 Makeevka
8 Voroshilovgrad
9 Taganrog
10 Engels
11 Ul'yanovsk
12 Tol'yatti

Population (thousands) Less than 500   500   1,000   2,000   5,000   10,000

Cities which are today subject to some form of industrial and demographic restriction include almost all cities with populations of over 500,000 and several smaller towns. The most comprehensive listing is given by B.S.Khorev *Problemy gorodov*, Moscow,1975, p.86. City population totals are for 1st January,1984.

*Sources:* Tsentral'noe Statisticheskoe Upravlenie SSSR (1984) *Narodnoe Khozyaistvo SSSR v 1983g.*, Finansy i Statistika, Moscow. pp. 18–23; B. S. Khorev (1975) *Problemy Gorodov*, Moscow.

0   km   1000

documentation or will allow a migrant to use his or her newly found 'place of work' as their 'place of residence' and so qualify for a *propiska*. In the labour-short Transcaucasian city of Baku, designated a 'closed city', it has recently been commented upon that factory managers and the city authorities permit workers to register as 'residents of their plants and factories' even though they do not have a place to live within the city. At the city's Volodarsky garment factory some 650 employees have given their workplace as their 'place of residence' but do not live there. Instead, such workers, along with others who do not possess the necessary documentation, find themselves living in what has become known as a 'second' Baku:

> The city's outskirts and vacant areas have become filled with 'unauthorised structures' that go up overnight. This 'second' Baku is a distressing sight. The city puts up high fences around the shanty-towns. A commission has declared the shacks unfit for habitation. (*Sotsialisticheskaya industria*, 25 March 1987:2)

Another common way of obtaining a *propiska* involves an arranged marriage. By marrying a city resident, a migrant automatically qualifies for permanent city residency. An example of this practice appears in the following extract from Hedrick Smith's book, *The Russians*:

> Klara's family lived in a dingy little provincial town. She was desperate to avoid being sent there or to Siberia on government assignment as a teacher after graduation. She found it impossible to get a job in Moscow because she could not get registered for Moscow housing. But Klara hit upon the scheme of marrying a Moscow lad to qualify for city housing as a wife. One of her close friends told me that Klara paid 1,500 rubles for a bogus marriage to the brother of another friend, never planning to spend a single night with him. In fact, the groom ducked out quickly after the wedding ceremony. All Klara wanted was to use the marriage certification in her passport and six months of 'married life' to obtain her Moscow *propiska*, her residence permit.

As the demand for a place to live in large cities has continued unabated and as more closed cities appear on the map in an attempt to regulate the influx of labour into their cities, the passport-*propiska* system has contributed to the creation of a new pattern of migration, that of *step-wise migration*. In the past the norm was for rural residents to move directly into one of the country's major cities. Today this pattern of migration is only typical of the least developed regions – notably Soviet Central Asia – where also rural-to-urban migration is least hindered by the formalities of the passport-*propiska* system. In contrast, step-wise migration means that migration flows occur in stages; first, from the countryside to the small town, then from the small town to a large metropolitan suburb where employment is found in the large city, and finally, possibly a generation later, a person or member of a family may move into the large city. That the passport-*propiska* system is contributing to such a new pattern of migration is borne out by a number of studies. For instance, it was found that in some years around two-thirds of all rural persons arriving in Siberia's largest city, Novosibirsk, were denied permission to register for housing and to settle there; instead, many had to settle in nearby smaller towns (Zaslavskaya, 1970:266). In Baku, it is estimated that some 200,000 people are living on the outskirts of the city because they do not have the necessary residence permit to qualify for city housing (*Sotsialisticheskaya industria*, 25 March 1987:2).

## Labour shortages

The passport-*propiska* system, in attempting to ameliorate housing shortages in large cities and to encourage labour to remain in smaller towns and in the countryside where industry is encouraged to invest, has actually contributed to particular types of urban labour shortages.

Labour shortages in large cities are now of primary concern to Soviet policymakers. In the European cities in particular, this situation has been exacerbated by the general ageing of the population which in turn has contributed to the declining birth rate and to a fall in the number of young people able to take up city employment. Cities such as Moscow, Leningrad, Riga and Kiev are now coming perilously close to being unable to reproduce themselves through demographic means. This demand for supplemental city labour, however, is not uniform across the employment spectrum. Indeed, large cities are generally characterised by an over-concentration of those in professional and skilled employment. This is partly due to the changing nature of their urban economies where there is a higher concentration of jobs in science, scientific and technical services, government and administration, public education and health care, compared with smaller towns. But it is also a consequence of the reluctance of highly educated and skilled personnel to give up the benefits which accrue to living in large cities. There is little if any material incentive and every reason to stay given the higher standard of urban services and living conditions that large cities offer. Moreover, moving from the closed city to take up employment elsewhere, even on a temporary basis, has its problems. Leaving cities like Moscow for the purpose of meeting the chronic shortage of specialists in smaller and newer towns does not guarantee a right on return to housing and city residency.

There is a great need for unskilled and semiskilled labour in the large cities, and the practice of hiring out-of-town workers has become commonplace. Indeed, in some large cities, a new division of labour can now be detected with a predominance of native city dwellers in professional and skilled employment and recently arrived migrants filling most of the unskilled and semiskilled job vacancies. According to one report, this is evident in Leningrad where 'the overwhelming majority of Leningraders [graduating from eighth-year schools] become specialists, while more than half of the city workers are made up by those from outside' (*Pravda*, 21 January 1985:7). A large proportion of these 'new migrants' are made up of two social groupings, commuters and limit workers.

### Commuters

In the Soviet context commuting generally refers to workers who travel from the area immediately surrounding a major city, usually from a suburban zone, into that city to work. It does not just mean the usual daily travel from home to workplace although this is by far the most common form of commuting, but includes those who may only return at weekends and who live during the working week with relatives or in specially provided dormitory accommodation. Commuting in general and daily commuting in particular provide an increasingly important source of labour for the largest cities, and is rivalled only by direct migration.

Commuting to and from major cities from the surrounding areas is not a new phenomenon. It existed before the Second World War, when many agricultural workers used to work for part of the year in city factories, returning to their homelands at harvest time. It is however only over the past two decades that commuting has grown both in scale and in its importance to meeting shortfalls in the labour supply of large cities. In Moscow, half a million jobs are filled by those living in its suburban zone, thus constituting 10–12 percent of the city's labour force (Khorev, 1984). Despite its obvious size and pull, Moscow is not atypical. Most large cities have witnessed a similar growth in commuting. According to Sigov (1986), 'In the metropolises, 30–40 percent of the working people spend two hours a day commuting to and from work, and 5–12 percent spend more than two hours.'

The commuters are generally unskilled and semiskilled workers employed in the least desirable city jobs which demand the lowest qualifications, such as in textiles, food processing, and in construction. Denied a *propiska* and the right to housing in the city, they commute often long distances to work yet have few of the privileges from being a part of city life that their fellow city-workers enjoy.

### Limit workers

Another source of supplemental city labour has emerged through the practice of short-term work contracts being offered to non-city residents, who are issued with a temporary *propiska*. These workers are known as limit workers or *limitchiki*, so called because of the limited amount of additional hired labour that each industrial enterprise is officially allowed to hire from outside the city. Most limit workers come from the countryside. Khorev (1984) estimates that each year requests for 100,000 limit workers are made by Moscow's industrial enterprises. Unlike commuters, they live in the city but are usually provided with the most basic of accommodation by their factory employers. In spite of their poor living conditions and debarment from acquiring the necessary permanent residency requirement for a city apartment, most limit workers prefer to live and work in the large city than in their previous rural environment. The proportion of those leaving after their temporary permit expires, however, is relatively low (about one-third), so it would seem that temporary *propiski* can be renewed, a clear reflection of the importance of this source of labour to the city's economy.

Limit workers are recruited into what Khorev (1984) calls 'especially unappealing types of work', notably the factory assembly-line, construction and transport. These overwhelmingly young, single and male workers, no doubt due to their precarious residency qualifications, tend to work assiduously, surpassing set production quotas and plans. In performing what is judged as 'low status' work and living in the poorest and most cramped accommodation, they tend to be regarded by Muscovites and Leningraders as second-class citizens and are alienated from much of city life as a consequence.

## Urbanisation and social well-being

Where one lives in the Soviet Union is closely related to the quality of life typically offered to an individual, with the large cities in particular – the so-called 'closed cities' – providing the highest standards of living and as a consequence being the most desirable places in which to live. Access to residency in these most privileged places is regulated by a passport-*propiska* system which is used by 'closed city' authorities as a method of controlling the influx of city migrants and as a way of coping with housing shortages. We have also noted that despite such housing shortages, there is generally more accommodation available, and it is of a higher standard, in 'closed cities'. Moreover, in contrast to most other towns, 'closed cities' have a far higher concentration of services and a wider range of amenities, all of which contribute to a better quality of life for those privileged to live and work in the large city.

We get some idea of the uneven impact that the urbanisation process has had by locating the 'closed city' within the overall settlement structure. As Fig. 3.2 illustrates, besides the 'closed city' we can single

Fig. 3.2 The urbanisation of well-being in the Soviet Union.

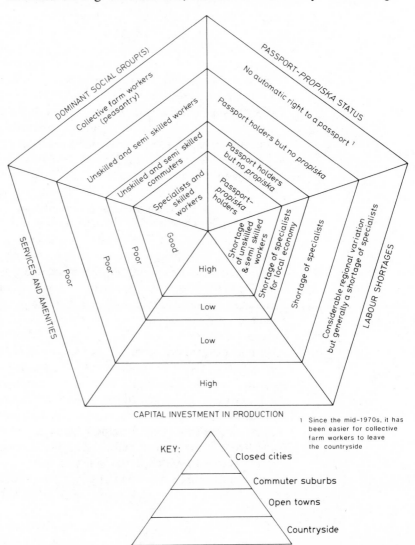

1 Since the mid-1970s, it has been easier for collective farm workers to leave the countryside

out three other types of settlement, each different from the others in the social opportunities and quality of life that it has to offer.

## Commuter suburbs

As a consequence of underurbanisation, the demand for housing in the large city has outstripped its available supply. Yet the demand for labour, particularly for unskilled and semiskilled employees, continues. This demand is partly filled by commuters who work in the large city but who, as late arrivals to big city life, are denied a city residence qualification. Commuters thus tend to live in less desirable housing in the outskirts or suburbs of the city where social amenities are spartan and the quality of life poor. Some even find it difficult to secure employment. Social problems linked to overcrowding, and to poorly equipped and impersonal apartment complexes, have emerged. Under such conditions, it is not surprising that one feature of many of these smaller, newly established towns with their large numbers of transient workers who have failed to secure their 'place in the sun', is the high crime-rate (Shelley, 1984). Much of this crime, however, is committed in the city rather than in the residential suburbs. According to one Soviet source, a recent feature of crime in Moscow involves organised 'cult gangs' of young males from the suburbs who come into the city at weekends with the explicit intention of 'beating-up' anyone who epitomises 'anti-Soviet tendencies', such as hippies and punk-rockers (*Ogonyok*, No. 5, January 1987:20–1). Labelled the 'Lyubery' (after Lyubertsy, a provincial suburb 19 kilometres south-east of Moscow), it has been suggested that part of the reason for their anti-social activity stems from the poorer services and facilities in many suburbs like Lyubertsy. Accordingly, 'their name [the "Lyubery"] has acquired the same negative connotation in Moscow schools as *limitchiki*' (*Sobesednik* No. 7, February 1987:10).

## 'Open towns'

Compared with 'closed cities', most small and medium-sized towns can be labelled 'open towns' because they do not carry the same residency qualifications other than possession of a passport. As we have noted, these towns suffer from underinvestment from the industrial ministries. Another feature is their limited provision of public services, poorer further education facilities, and fewer amenities. They thus constitute environments which are far from conducive to the creation of a highly skilled workforce or to the attraction of much-needed specialists from elsewhere. The labour force of 'open towns' therefore tends to be largely unskilled and semiskilled. Their economy is often dominated by one major industrial enterprise or plant. In a situation like this, workers have little alternative but to work and live in the town. Employment in the 'closed city', where their labour is in demand, is an alternative but without a *propiska* it is difficult. Moreover, in those towns where there is an overabundance of unskilled labour (in part due to the problems of attracting more industrial investment), the phenomenon of 'hidden unemployment', particularly among women, has emerged, in which due to the lack of jobs married women who have previously worked are forced into staying at home.

### The countryside

Finally, there are the collective farm workers or peasantry who constitute the majority of the rural population. Despite the 1974 passport reforms, their right to receive a passport and thus, if they so wish, to leave the countryside has only recently been fully realised. It was at the discretion of the local party as to whether a collective farm worker was to be issued with a passport. As a consequence, the passport continued to regulate the exodus from the countryside. Although standards of living and social opportunities for the peasantry have improved considerably over the past two decades in particular, they still lag well behind those of their urban counterparts, whether measured in terms of income, educational facilities, shops, nurseries or health service provision. For instance, the average family in the town spends far more on consumer durables than a rural family, and twice as much on services. Measured against the city, then, the countryside has less to offer its inhabitants. It is therefore not surprising that it is particularly the young and most gifted who constitute the bulk of rural migrants and who rarely return with their city diplomas to work in the countryside.

As for the rural economy, which we will consider in more detail in chapter 6, you will recall that under Stalin, state investment in both agricultural production and in rural infrastructure was neglected for the sake of rapid industrialisation. This led to serious consequences for agricultural output and productivity which successive leaders since the mid-1950s have attempted to rectify by investing large amounts of capital in the rural economy. Yet, as we shall see, this has only dented the surface; agriculture, not least because of its inefficiency, now constitutes one-quarter of state investment, making it the single largest item in budgetary expenditure.

### Summary

In this chapter we have argued that the most significant feature of urbanisation in the USSR is underurbanisation. City growth has been uneven, with the large cities in particular increasing at a far faster pace primarily due to the spatial pattern of industrial investment. This has meant that there is a considerable demand in the largest cities for additional labour. In order to cope with increased demand for housing and services in large cities, the state's response has been to regulate new factory development and labour migration. Restricting migration into the large cities has involved the use of the passport-*propiska* system. Yet the state's limited success in encouraging industry to move to smaller towns has meant that the demand in the large cities for industrial labour in particular continues to grow. Under these circumstances, the restrictions on city residency have meant that a large proportion of this needed additional labour is made up of commuters and limit workers, both being social groups which do not enjoy the same right of residency as natives of the large cities. Urbanisation has also produced a settlement hierarchy of social well-being, with the residents of large cities enjoying privileges which are denied to most other communities, owing to the existence of the passport-*propiska* system.

# 4 Regional policy and regional development

In a country as diverse as the Soviet Union, it is not surprising that issues of regional development have long been of concern to planners and policymakers. The general consensus on such issues is that it is the responsibility of the state and its planning organs to work towards the more balanced development of the regions, with the socially and economically backward being singled out for special treatment. To this end, the goal of regional development is clear: to facilitate the planned development of the regions in order to reduce and eventually to eradicate inter-regional disparties. Within the economic sphere, however, regional development has invariably been fashioned far more by exogenous pressures and by structural features associated with the planning process than by considerations of regional equalisation. For example, during the Second World War, regions east of the Urals, notably Western Siberia, were singled out for rapid industrial development for purely defensive reasons. Within the arena of planning also, with its emphasis on allocating capital investment between sectors of the economy rather than on a regional basis, regions tend to fare accordingly. Yet which regions should receive priority and how they should be developed within the framework of the national economy have become highly contestable issues. In this chapter we examine the dilemmas facing policymakers and planners concerning the regions and the processes which have shaped their development. Particular attention will be paid to what has been described as the world's largest underdeveloped region, Siberia. The issues surrounding its past and future development and the constraints and stimuli working towards its more balanced integration into the national economy will be examined.

## Regional policy and problem regions

Few countries match the scale of regional development problems that confront the Soviet Union. Many of these emanate from the country's sheer regional diversity and from the need to coordinate marked imbalances in the factors of production characteristic of its three macro regions: European USSR, Siberia (including the Far East), and Central Asia (Table 4.1). Each of these regions tends to have particular problems which may be the reverse of problems found in other regions. Specifically these include inter-regional inequalities in the labour supply, the availability of energy and raw material resources, and the level of development of the physical and social infrastructure. These variations also highlight two essential dualisms of the Soviet regional problem: west and east, and north and south.

The European part of the country possesses all the ingredients of a mature industrial society: a well-developed industrial base and

**Table 4.1 Disparities in the factors of production for the USSR's macro regions**

| | Factors | |
|---|---|---|
| **Regions** | Positive | Negative |
| European USSR | Established industrial base<br>Well-developed physical and<br>  social infrastructure<br>Skilled labour force | Labour shortages<br>Scarce fuels and raw material<br>  resources |
| Siberia | Abundance of fuels and raw<br>  materials | Labour shortages<br>Underdeveloped social<br>  infrastructure<br>Transportation costs<br>Inhospitable physical<br>  environment |
| Central Asia | Labour surplus<br>Fuel and raw material resources | Unskilled and immobile labour<br>  force<br>Lack of factory tradition<br>Underdeveloped physical and<br>  social infrastructure |

economic infrastructure, and a skilled labour force. In containing about three-quarters of the Soviet population, it has the largest national market and the highest returns on investment capital. By becoming a fully industrialised economy, however, the region has had to rely increasingly on additional sources of energy and raw materials which has meant a growing dependency on natural-resource-rich Siberia. This latter region contains 90 percent of the country's fossil fuels (and 15 percent of the world's). As a consequence, the USSR is the only major industrialised country in the world that is independent in energy. Yet underdeveloped and underpopulated as Siberia is, the region has had continually to rely on labour from west of the Urals in order to develop and diversify its extractive-based economy. Since the early 1960s, however, this surplus of European labour has begun to dry up. As labour shortages are now a 'northern' rather than just a Siberian problem, planners have been looking towards the country's third-world region, Central Asia, for additional labour. Here population growth continues and there is now a substantial rural surplus. But the problem is that Central Asia's population is largely unskilled and notoriously immobile, reluctant even to move into its region's local cities let alone settle in the north. Despite also possessing a substantial energy and raw material base, planners have been reluctant to switch more than a limited amount of capital investment from European USSR. In short, limited returns from investment work to Central Asia's disadvantage.

Which regions should receive priority in order to overcome these mismatches in production is therefore the central problem facing policymakers and planners. In arriving at such decisions as embodied in the Plan document, decision-takers claim to be guided by a number of underlying principles or 'laws' of development. These 'laws' are derived from the works of Marx, Engels and Lenin, and by decisions taken at various Party Congresses. They are as follows:

1  Enterprises should be located as near as possible to raw material sources and to centres of production.

2   Economic activity should be distributed throughout the whole country.
3   There should be a rational distribution of labour between regions and the 'complex development' of the economy of each region.
4   The economic and cultural levels of the least developed nationality areas should be raised to those of the most advanced.
5   The distinction between town and country should be eliminated.
6   The defence potential of the country should be strengthened.
7   There should be an international division of labour in the socialist bloc (Comecon) countries.

What is particularly apparent from an examination of these laws is that many form the basis for locational decision making in non-socialist countries (e.g. law 1). Indeed, considerable interest was shown by early Soviet industrial location theorists in the works of the neo-classical economist, Alfred Weber, better known for his ideas on Western location theory. Although Weber's ideas were subsequently denounced as of no relevance to socialist planning, none the less the ideas that he advanced on minimalising transport costs can be detected in the first law of socialist development. This is not surprising given the vast distances that the new regime inherited between natural resources (Siberia) and centres of consumption (European USSR). Other 'laws', however, are unique to the socialist world (e.g. law 7). It is also evident that many of these laws appear to be contradictory (e.g. laws 1 and 2). In practice, what this has meant is that locational decisions have tended to be fashioned in accordance with those laws most appropriate to the economic, political and geo-strategic circumstances of the moment. For example, as we noted in the introduction, with increasing likelihood of war with Germany in the late 1930s, the thrust of regional policy was towards the dispersal of industrial investment to the Urals and West Siberia, and away from the geo-strategically vulnerable industrial centres of European USSR, particularly the Donbass. (This was reflected in increased state investment in Siberia and the Far East in the 1938–45 period, as shown in Fig. 4.1.)

Decisions over regional and sectoral investment become that much more political as a consequence. As we noted in chapter 1, to varying degrees depending on their political muscle, interest groups can play a part in influencing both Plan construction, the actual Plan document, and the extent to which the Plan is translated into practice. Ministries lobby on behalf of their industries' needs and development programmes while regional and city officials argue for those programmes which are likely to benefit their respective localities. Indeed, as in most countries concerned with regional development, tension exists between those who favour the evening out of regional differences through policies of *dispersing* investment resources to the less developed regions, and those groups favouring the more efficient and effective use of investment through its continuing *concentration* in well-established regions. The particular issue will determine the actual composition of alliances but generally the latter invariably comprises a formidable lobby made up of most of the industrial ministries and European regional and local interest groups. Representatives of the less developed regions, smaller cities and other local groupings generally comprise the opposing camp. No other issue has been so hotly debated as the question of Siberia's development.

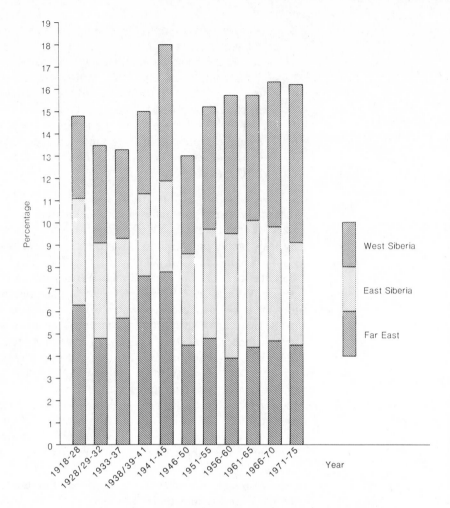

Fig. 4.1 Percentage share of Soviet investment in Siberia and its regions, 1918–75.

*Source:* Data from B. Rumer (1984) *Investment and Reindustrialisation in the Soviet Economy*, Boulder, Westview, pp. 68–9.

### Siberia: 'complex' or 'limited' development?

The formation of the modern Siberian economy owes much to three developments in particular. The first concerns the region's role during the Stalin years as a repository for forced labour. There is little doubt that the region's rapid development, particularly the exploitation of its raw-material base and the establishment of its southern manufacturing belt, owes much to the deployment and use of GULag labour.

The second stimulus came from what is often identified as heralding a regional policy, the 1930s construction of the Urals-Kuznetsk *combinat*. This was a huge project of inter-regional resource integration for the production of steel, based on supplies of iron ore from the Urals (Magnitogorsk) and coking coal from the Kuzbass (Kuznetsk). Until recently, the considered opinion was that the underlying reason for developing this metallurgical base was taken primarily for economic reasons premissed on the Weberian logic of building up a manufacturing base near the source of raw materials and so minimalising transport costs. More recent evidence, however, suggests that from an economic standpoint, the decision was wholly irrational. Even as early as 1928, the Soviet economist, Dimanshtein, was arguing that the transportation costs required to combine Ural iron ore with Kuzbass coal would be so high that they would outweigh the lower mining costs of these raw materials. Indeed, it was later discovered that the chemical composition of Kuzbass coal was inadequate for high-quality Ural iron ore. This was later to lead to the development of the Karaganda coal basin. But rather than interpreting this as an inefficient decision taken at the top, other evidence suggests that defensive considerations were the main motive. Certainly much of the leadership's rhetoric in the late 1920s contained reference for the need to disperse industry away from strategically vulnerable European USSR, and more specifically to reduce the national economy's dependence on its only large metallurgical base in the Donbass. It was a decision which was to be followed in the late 1930s by the build-up of industry in Western Siberia and the Urals as the country prepared to defend its western borders.

The third stimulus to the region's development concerns its exploitation as a resource base for European USSR. Continuing demand from the country's industrial heartland to supplement raw material and energy resources from its own progressively depleting resource base has resulted in the further opening up of Siberia. In the early 1960s, the oil and gas fields of Tyumen *oblast* were developed, followed in the 1970s by large-scale capital investment in the extraction of the rich deposits of lignite from the Kansk-Achinsk field. These decisions were taken largely from the standpoint that in a region where labour shortages act as a brake on development and in which the state no longer has forced labour to draw upon, Siberia was to be developed along more 'limited' lines.

Yet since the inception of central planning and the Five Year Plan, the country's 'eastern frontier' has been described as ripe for development. No major shift in funding, however, has been forthcoming in the post-war period. Between 1951 and 1975, each FYP directive offered verbal support for more rapid eastern development, but the actual share of total investment going to Siberia was virtually constant at between 15 and 17 percent (Fig. 4.1). It was not until the early 1980s that it reached 20 percent. Supporters of investment in European USSR, a coalition of regional interests and the industrial ministries, have managed to stabilise the situation in spite of the verbal emphasis given to opening up the Eastlands. It is therefore the state's degree of commitment to the more balanced and 'complex' development of the region which has been questioned both inside and outside the Soviet Union.

## The pro-Siberian lobby

This pressure group, made up of local and regional officials, planners, and academics from the influential Novosibirsk Economics Institute, has been particularly active since the 1960s in arguing for the region's more complex development. Much is made of the limited potential of European USSR's energy and raw material resources and of the future prosperity of the national economy lying with the utilisation of Siberia's resources. While it is acknowledged that Siberia has higher construction and labour costs, it is also argued that these are more than offset by far cheaper extraction and exploitation costs (e.g. cheaper coal from Kansk-Achinsk and from hydro-electric power). But the Siberian lobby does not see the region as functioning merely as a

53

'fossil fuel colony' of European USSR. While it is also conceded that at present long-haulage and cross-haulage costs are high, the further development of the region's manufacturing base, so it is argued, would reduce such costs as well as lift much of the strain off an already overburdened transportation system. But a more balanced and modern economy cannot be achieved while Moscow continues to economise on the region's social infrastructure. More funding is needed, it is argued, for housing and services in order to utilise the region's full potential and to attract and retain a labour force which in the past has acted as a brake on regional economic growth.

### The pro-European lobby

A formidably powerful European lobby comprising most of the well-entrenched big industrial ministries and regional and local representatives west of the Urals questions the logic behind the further and more balanced development of Siberia. However, this grouping should not be judged so much as being anti-Siberian as pro-European. First, while accepting the continuing significance that Siberian fossil fuels and raw materials make to the country's well-being, it questions the merit of scarce investment resources being channelled into a region where there is little short-term return and where long-term benefit to the national economy is doubtful. It is noted with concern that as a result of recent large-scale and often grandiose capital-intensive projects, Siberia has become a major consumer of capital investment. Throughout the 1960s and early 1970s in particular, the region received well over the USSR average per caput investment, with Siberia's major regions receiving between 145 and 149 percent of the Soviet norm for the 1971–75 period. Second, it is suggested from the standpoint of the contribution of European USSR to the Soviet economy generally, that investment would be far more effectively used west of the Urals. Much is made of the need to revitalise the older industrialised parts of European USSR like the Donbass, an argument which has clearly won favour in Moscow. Thus from the 1970s onwards, capital investment has tended to be channelled into the rebuilding and expansion of existing industrial enterprises rather than into the establishment of new enterprises which are important to the development of a younger Siberian economy. Whereas in 1970, 58 percent of all funds allocated to industrial investment were targeted for renovation and expansion of older enterprises, by 1980 this had risen sharply to 72 percent (Rumer, 1984). Last, there is the 'East European factor' to consider. The point that considerable advantages exist for European USSR owing to its proximity to the socialist states of Eastern Europe, has not been lost on those with vested interests. This has already been recognised in the increased integration of European USSR with Eastern Europe. Most notable has been the development and further proposed expansion of the Kursk Magnetic Anomaly in European USSR, the USSR's second largest deposit of iron ore. The export of iron from Kursk to Eastern Europe is to be reduced and to be partly replaced by the more economical export of semi-finished iron and steel products manufactured in European USSR. This will reduce the high costs of hauling large volumes of low-value iron ore to Eastern Europe.

## Sub-regional strategies

While on balance Siberia has tended to lose out to European USSR, it would be wrong to suggest that this diverse region is simply treated in an undifferentiated way. A far more complex picture of development has emerged in which sub-regions have been singled out for particular types of development. Two examples illustrate this.

The first example concerns the Pacific seaboard. With the USSR's increasing integration into the world economy since the 1960s, policymakers have not been slow to recognise the significance of the Pacific seaboard's proximity to Western markets, specifically to Japan and the United States. From as early as the mid-1960s, a series of major Soviet-Japanese trade agreements were signed concerning the exploitation and processing of Soviet timber and the export of coal. In return, the Soviet Union received Japanese industrial goods. This gave substantial stimulus to the development of the Pacific seaboard and resulted in the refurbishment of the port of Nakhodka and the creation of another at Vostochnyi. The significance of the region to Western markets was also one reason for the building of the Baykal-Amur Mainline (BAM) which it was argued would facilitate further international trade as well as provide an outlet for the rich raw materials and timber reserves opened up by the BAM. However, the extent to which foreign capital will help to further stimulate the region's economy is highly dependent on global politics and upon *détente* between the superpowers. The now defunct Yakutia Gas Project illustrates this problem. This 1970s scheme for transporting

The Yankan Pass, one of the most difficult sectors in the building of the Baykal-Amur Mainline railway.

Siberian natural gas eastwards for export in liquid form via Vanino to Japan and the United States was abandoned precisely because of the hotting-up of the Cold War towards the end of that decade. But the idea of drawing upon Western capital to finance the region's long-term development is one which must be attractive to a Soviet leadership that is also more conscious of the country's increasing role within the world economy. Whether Moscow is prepared to go as far as the Chinese by establishing a Special Economic Zone as the basis to attract direct foreign investment is too early to tell.

The second example concerns the development of the West Siberian oil and gas complex in Tyumen *oblast.* This area contains by far the richest oil and gas reserves in the country and now accounts for well over half of all Soviet oil and gas production. The strategy here has been one of specialised development based on the export of oil and gas via an increasingly complex network of pipelines to consumers in European USSR and Comecon. The bulk of investment goes into oil and gas extraction and into developing those branches of industry connected with the initial stages of the production cycle. The labour attracted by the region's high wages records a high turnover, in part due to underinvestment in social infrastructure. For instance, during a crucial period in the region's development (1965–75), population growth was 1.3 times higher than the rate of capital investment in social infrastructure. While West Siberian vested interests in particular have questioned the merits of the region's overspecialisation and bemoaned its limited diversity, the major issue of the 1980s concerns whether further investment should go into tapping the region's considerable oil and gas reserves.

Questions over the region's future contribution to the Soviet

Blocks of workers' flats in the oil city of Surgut, Tyumen *oblast.*

economy are essentially to do with whether the USSR should invest more resources in coal, atomic energy and hydro-electric power or in oil and gas. By 1980, the debate had reached something of a climax. The oil and gas lobby formed a relatively cohesive group. It included various ministries with ties to the oil and gas industries, the head of Gosplan, and local Tyumen interests. That West Siberia also received support from other oil- and gas-producing regions, which also contain high concentrations of oil- and gas-related industries (e.g. chemical, automobile, aircraft) is in part explained by their reliance on West Siberia generating the wealth through export of oil and gas which would be used to purchase specialised oil and gas equipment to help exploitation from these older producing regions.

The opposition to further investment in the production of the region's oil and gas industry was weakened by its lack of unity. The coal lobby in particular had also come in for criticism. Throughout the 1970s, a disproportionate rise had occurred in mining costs. In European USSR, coal has had to be mined from greater and greater depths and now some of it is no longer of a high quality. Moreover, in 1980, the leadership of the coal industry was singled out for its poor management and inability to arrest either declining production or falling labour productivity. In contrast, investment costs in oil and gas tended to be more quickly recovered than in coal.

In 1980, the Politburo made the final policy decision in favour of oil and gas production: Tyumen was to be provided with adequate capital and equipment. Since then, however, the industry has met with mixed fortunes. Gas production in Tyumen is to be trebled at least until the end of the century, while oil output is to be maintained at the present level. There seem to be two main reasons behind this lower priority for oil production. First, there is the cost of exploration and extraction which is high in comparison with most other energy sources. Linked to this is the underdeveloped nature of oil extraction technology. Secondly, it has been argued that considerable benefits would accrue in the long term to conserving reserves for future generations. As a consequence, oil deliveries to Comecon countries have been reduced and oil exports to third world countries have almost ceased. Instead there is a re-emphasis on nuclear power. Some 70 percent of the total growth in electrical generating capacity is to come from a projected doubling of the share of nuclear power between 1985 (10 percent) and 1990 (21 percent). Most of this increase in capacity is to come from European USSR's nuclear power industry where much-needed additional energy can be found without incurring high transport costs. In spite of environmentalist opposition to an industry which in 1986 experienced the world's worst ever nuclear power accident at Chernobyl in the Ukraine, the government, in accepting the accident's cause as due to improper management rather than design flaws, points to the need for cheaper nuclear power in meeting the growing industrial demands of European USSR and Comecon.


**Constraint to development: the regional labour supply**

The major problem facing planners with regard to Siberia's development is labour shortages. This problem is of course not new but as the region's contribution to the national economy has grown, so has its apparently insatiable demand for outside labour. Ironically, while Stalin's forced labour policies guaranteed an eastward flow of population, the subsequent policies, based on enticing labour to settle in Siberia through wage and other material benefits, have met with more limited success. The problem of attracting labour to Siberia, however, has entered a new phase as a result of its dependency on a steadily decreasing European workforce. Estimates for the 1986–90 period suggest a 0.6 percent decrease (or one million fewer workers) in the country's labour supply. This is primarily due to the falling birth rate in European USSR which began in the early 1960s and the now fewer people entering the region's labour force (Perevedentsev, 1982). Siberia's traditional regional reservoir of labour is now unable to meet the needs of European USSR let alone those of Siberia.

The state has a number of means to encourage labour migration at its disposal. As a centrally planned economy, the state can determine through investment policy the nature and location of jobs, and seek to provide for the consequent demand for labour. One relatively recent innovation has been the use of employment bureaus which attempt to match available labour and skills to locational demand. Central planners also plan wage rates and use other material inducements to encourage labour to move to those places earmarked for industrial development. Yet the problem is that labour does not necessarily move to those places which the government views as desirable. As in Western economies, individuals literally vote with their feet by moving (or not  moving) to the place they judge best fulfils their needs. What this in effect means is that there is considerable unplanned migration which presents problems for an economy planning regional development.

In assessing the problems associated with centrally directed labour migration, two such schemes can be singled out: planned migration schemes and regional wage differentials. The most established of the planned migration schemes is *orgnabor* (the organised recruitment of labour). It dates back to the early 1930s and has been responsible for relocating some 30 million people, mainly for employment in Siberian industry and in construction projects. It operates through a fixed-term contract system (the minimum is one year) for which recruits are offered a variety of bonuses and inducements for relocation. Amongst its predominantly young and single male recruits, turnover remains high, suggesting that incentives are not sufficient to offset more permanent settlement. The scheme's contribution to Siberia's labour force has also declined sharply since the mid-1950s as it has become increasingly involved in more localised project recruitment. A second scheme, operated by *Komsomol* (The Young Communist League) is less structured (there is no fixed contract). It is designed to appeal to youthful romanticism and itchy feet but was never intended to encourage permanent resettlement. It continues to have a Siberian focus (it was particularly active in recruitment for such large-scale projects as the building of the Baykal-Amur Mainline and other Siberian development schemes in Urengoi and Ust-Illimsk). Finally, there is the graduate placement scheme. After completing a higher or specialised education, graduates are required to accept compulsory (usually three-year) placement. In the past, this scheme provided the region with a pool of highly trained labour but as the state has become more sensitive to individual wishes, assignments to Siberia have declined.

One of the major problems to emerge with these schemes is in effectively matching locational demand with the required quantity and quality of labour. It is often the case that migration schemes lack information from labour-short areas on employment openings and on the particular skills required. This clearly hampers the effective planned redistribution of the labour force. In order to resolve this problem, a new administrative organisation was set up in 1977 to oversee and coordinate organised migration. This State Commission for Labour and Social Problems (*Goskomtrud*) has responsibility over a number of the organised migration channels (e.g. *orgnabor*, the new employment bureaus, job transfers), as well as having the job of overseeing the graduate placement scheme and Komsomol appeals. It is hoped that with greater centralisation and liaison between these schemes, the particular needs of regions and sectors of the economy will be more fully realised.

In addition to the above, centrally fixed regional wage differentials now operate which are designed in particular to encourage labour migration to Siberia and the Northlands (Fig. 4.2). Workers in designated regions are entitled to a percentage increase in monthly salary, calculated according to a spatially differentiated regional coefficient. The function of this coefficient is simple: to compensate workers for regional variations in the cost of living which generally tend to be higher the further east and north a worker is prepared to

Fig. 4.2 Regional wage coefficients and supplements in the USSR.

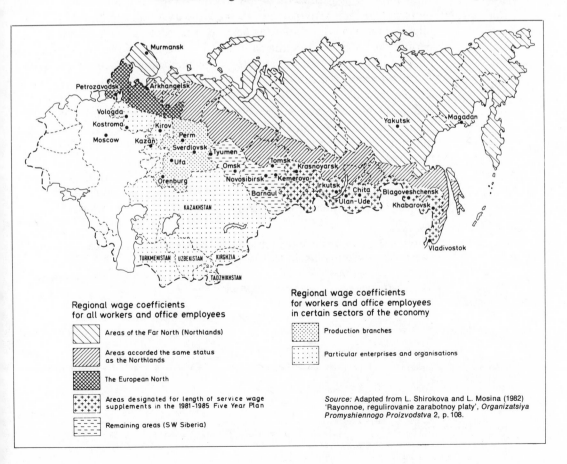

Regional wage coefficients
for all workers and office employees

Areas of the Far North (Northlands)

Areas accorded the same status as the Northlands

The European North

Areas designated for length of service wage supplements in the 1981-1985 Five Year Plan

Remaining areas (SW Siberia)

Regional wage coefficients
for workers and office employees
in certain sectors of the economy

Production branches

Particular enterprises and organisations

*Source:* Adapted from L. Shirokova and L. Mosina (1982) 'Rayonnoe, regulirovanie zarabotnoy platy', *Organizatsiya Promyshiennogo Proizvodstva* 2, p. 108.

settle. Up until recently, such extra payments included only the northern parts of Siberia and European USSR. But in response to the continuing southward and westward demand for additional labour, regional wage coefficients were extended in the 1981–85 plan period to include workers and office employees in the Urals, parts of Kazakhstan, and in the north European provinces of Vologda and Kirov. In addition, a series of so-called *osnovnyye* privileges exists to make work in a given locality more attractive. These include a system of periodical 'northern' inducements to basic pay, supplementary leave (*otpusk*) each year (eighteen working days in the extreme North), and certain accommodation benefits. A wage supplement for uninterrupted service in these designated regions, offered to attract long-term settlement, has also recently been extended to include the southern manufacturing belt of East Siberia and the Far East. In short, the map of planned wage differentials and other regional inducements has become more extensive and complex, with some Siberian provinces, like Tomsk and Irkutsk, offering as many as five different wage differentials for working in particular locations and sectors of their economies (Shirokova and Mosina, 1982).

## The problem of labour turnover

The problem is not simply one of attracting labour to Siberia but of actually retaining it once it has settled there. There has however been some improvement since the 1960s when most areas of Siberia lost more people than arrived there. In the years 1970–80, the flow of migration leaving Siberia fell by 66.7 percent, while in the 1975–80 period, the balance of migration in East Siberia and the Far East was positive. The term used to describe this phenomenon is *labour turnover*. For our purposes, it can be defined as the proportion of workers leaving their place of employment for elsewhere. Siberia's labour force has the highest turnover in the country, and turnover is 50 percent higher than in European USSR. While much of this turnover involves migrants leaving the region, there is also considerable intra-regional turnover. As a study of the potential mobility of urban workers in Siberia shows (Table 4.2), marginally more workers felt that they were likely to change their employment but remain in the region (18.4 percent of those interviewed), compared with 17.4 percent who said

**Table 4.2  The potential mobility, by percentage, of urban workers in West Siberia in 1984**

| Migration intentions | Employment intentions | | | Total |
|---|---|---|---|---|
| | Will or may change job | Will not change job | Unsure | |
| Will or may leave | 17.4 | — | 1.5 | 18.9 |
| Will not leave | 18.4 | 49.0 | 2.8 | 70.2 |
| Unsure | 4.9 | 5.3 | 0.7 | 10.9 |
| Total | 40.7 | 54.3 | 5.0 | 100.0 |

*Source:* V. Zaslavskaya, V. Kalmyk and L. Khakhulina (1986) 'Problemy sotsial'nogo razvitiya Sibiri puti ikh resheniya', *Izvestiya Sibirskogo otdeleniya Akademii nauk SSSR. Seriya Ekonomiki i prikladnoi sotsiologii* 1, pp. 36.45.

they were likely to leave Siberia. Turnover is also selective; how long a worker has been resident in a given place is one determinant. Thus in a survey of employees in two of the major cities in the Kansk-Achinsk coalfield, of the fifth of all those who planned to leave the city, the majority were 'new settlers' (those resident for less than ten years) (Nozdrina, 1982). Turnover also tends to be sectorally specific with particularly high levels being recorded for workers in the more transient oil and gas industries, and in construction.

There are a number of reasons why labour turnover is so high in spite of wage and other incentives. While increases in Siberian salaries have had an impact in reducing labour turnover (an increase was recorded of between 1.7 and 2.0 percent in 1970–82 relative to other regions), they do not compensate for the region's higher cost of living. (In order to absorb transport costs, many imported foods and other consumer items are dearer. The average family budget has also to allocate more for heating and warm clothing.) As a number of Soviet economists have argued, without linking regional wages to the actual cost of living, workers are unlikely to move and settle on a more permanent basis.

It is not so much wages and salaries which are cited by would-be migrants as reasons for leaving as the lack of consumer goods, amenities and services (Table 4.3). The quality and shortage of housing, together with limited health care and fewer schools, are cited as the primary reasons for labour dissatisfaction. These problems are particularly acute in the countryside. The underfinancing of such services and amenities also makes it that much more unpalatable to have to put up with Siberia's harsh physical environment. But even with higher earnings, there is the problem of actually being able to spend wages. Indeed there has been a growing trend in the imbalance between the population's monetary income and the availability of basic consumer goods. The deterioration in the average diet of the Siberian population, for instance, has been linked to periodic shortages of fruit and vegetables. It is therefore not surprising that the Siberian workforce

**Table 4.3  Reasons cited by potential migrants in West Siberia for leaving the region (percentage figures)**

| Reasons | Rural workers | | | Urban workers |
|---|---|---|---|---|
| | 1967 | 1977 | 1982 | 1984 |
| Housing conditions | 6 | 8 | 21 | 15 |
| Climatic conditions | 3 | 5 | 1 | 21 |
| Lack of provision of goods and services | 17 | 19 | 15 | 15 |
| Lack of cultural and educational facilities | 3 | 3 | 6 | 12 |
| Conditions of work | 16 | 19 | 22 | 5 |
| Salary and wages | 7 | 2 | 3 | 6 |
| Family and health reasons | 8 | 13 | 16 | 20 |
| Way of life in general | 13 | 6 | 2 | 0 |
| Other factors (including unspecified responses) | 27 | 27 | 14 | 6 |

*Source:* V. Zaslavskaya, V. Kalmyk and L. Khakhulina (1986) 'Problemy sotsial'nogo razvitiya Sibiri puti ikh resheniya', *Izvestiya Sibirskogo otdeleniya Akademii nauk SSSR. Seriya Ekonomiki i prikladnoi sotsiologii* 1, pp. 36–45.

has one of the highest levels of personal savings in the country. This tendency to save, however, is not just a product of limited spending power. It also reflects a particular type of worker attracted to Siberia's higher earnings economy who goes there with the explicit intention of returning home with a large savings account.

Given that labour is likely to remain a scarce commodity into the foreseeable future, ways must be found to meet such a shortfall. Instead of relying on outside labour, it is likely that greater emphasis will be given to the more effective utilisation of Siberia's existing workforce. This becomes especially critical given the region's move towards more intensive development and the resulting demand for more skilled labour. At present, its workforce possesses lower educational qualifications than that in European USSR. One way of building up a pool of skilled labour would be by increasing and improving institutions for technical training. Also, those sectors of the economy concerned with the region's future development could be more effectively coordinated and tied more closely into territorial planning. One attempt at improving labour productivity by this means and so making more effective use of existing labour is through the establishment of territorial production complexes, which are considered below. Certainly poor coordination at the intra-regional level between various institutional interests involved in the production process often affects labour productivity. According to a recent survey of Siberian workers, four-fifths stated that they would work harder and more productively if there was an improvement in the supply of equipment and materials, as well as in working conditions and in the organisation of work (Zaslavskaya, Kalmyk and Khakhulina, 1986). Finally, as local industrial enterprises are now beginning to acknowledge, there is a considerable demand by migrants to increase their personal income by taking on a second job. This would provide at least a temporary solution to labour shortages.

## Stimulus to development: Territorial Production Complexes

One of the most innovative attempts to reduce labour turnover in Siberia and to coordinate the various institutions involved in the local production process has been the setting-up of Territorial Production Complexes (TPCs). The TPC is based on the notion that central to regional development is linking sectoral planning with territorial planning in a way that will facilitate the development of economic activities in selected regions.

Over the past decade in particular, the TPC has become a familiar feature of the Soviet industrial landscape and reflects the greater significance given to more effective planned regional development. The vast majority of TPCs are to be found in the less developed regions of the country, particularly in Siberia and the Northlands (Fig. 4.3). They have attracted the support of the Siberian lobby who see the TPC as holding the key to the region's future.

Since the geographer, Kolosovsky, first advocated the idea of regionally based and integrated production cycles back in the 1920s, the notion of the TPC has undergone substantial revision to the extent that there are now numerous definitions and prescriptions.

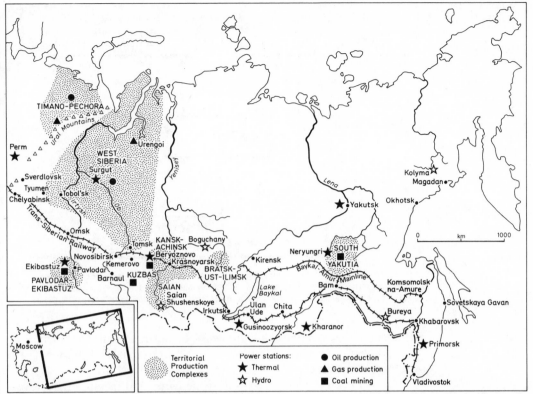

*Source:* K. Spidchenko (1984) *Geografiya XI Pyatiletki*, Moscow.

Fig. 4.3 Territorial Production Complexes (TPCs) in Siberia and the Northlands.

Barabasheva (1980:42) provides one of the clearest definitions:

A TPC is a group of industries in various sectors within a circumscribed geographical area, united for the purpose of all-round development and joint use of this area and its natural and labour resources in the interests of the nation's economy, and of the joint efficient use of the economic and social infrastructure.

The following 'elements', summarised in diagrammatic form in Fig. 4.4, form the basic structure of a TPC, and are the main elements to be considered in the complex's effective territorial planning:

1 *Production* The production structure of a TPC consists of a combination of *specialised* and *diversified* industries. It is however around a specialised industry or set of industries – usually mining and manufacturing – that more diversified economic activity is developed. These diversified industries, in turn, reflect local resource strengths and economic feasibility. One example is oil and gas production in the West Siberian TPC which forms the basis of the complex's specialised economy and which also contributes significantly to the national economy (as well as to Comecon). These specialised industries also form the basis of the TPC's diversification through developments like the petrochemical complex at Tobol'sk and the electric power station at Surgut. Unlike specialised production activities, auxiliary production is largely intended for regional rather than national consumption, although many of these more minor industries do export to other regions. What then will determine the specialised nature of a TPC will be such factors as the complex's resources, given national demand for

63

Fig. 4.4   The main elements of
a TPC.

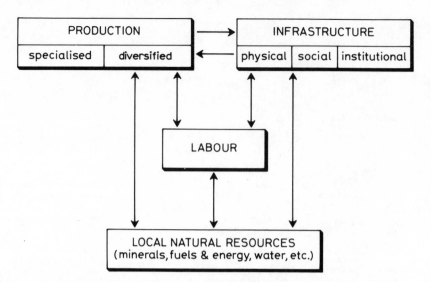

*Source:* Modified from M. Bandman (1976) 'Towards improving the content, procedures and
tools of optimization in pre-plan research', in M. Bandman (ed.) *Regional Development in the
USSR. Modelling the formation of Soviet Territorial Production Complexes*, Pergamon, Oxford,
p. 14.

them, the geographical conditions of the area, capital investment
and operating costs of production per unit output, and product
transportation costs to consumers.

2   *Infrastructure*   This refers to those activities and facilities that serve
the TPC and its population. For Siberia's development in
particular, giving infrastructure equal weight to production in the
planning equation is viewed as being one of the most constructive
aspects of the TPC. Three types of infrastructural support are
identified: physical (e.g. transport, pipelines, water supplies), social
(e.g. housing and utilities, services, schools), and institutional (e.g.
party and administrative authorities, higher educational and
specialised schools). Undoubtedly, the extent and quality of a
region's infrastructure influences the efficiency of production and the
labour situation. So it is imperative that the resources necessary for
infrastructural development are provided and planned for in a
forward-looking and coordinated fashion.

3   *Labour*   As the acknowledged key element to the productive and
consumptive functioning of a TPC, it is this factor more than any
other which is vital to its success. This is especially so given
Siberia's problems of attracting and stabilising its workforce, as we
have noted. Much therefore depends on whether the infrastructure
and environment of a TPC matches workers' aspirations. Its
composition (e.g. age, sex, education) will clearly be dependent on
the structure of productive activities and of the type of employment
required.

4   *Local natural resources*   These are a necessary precondition for
TPC formation. The realised potential of a region's resources – be
they minerals, fuels and energy, water or land – will be dependent
on the relative costs of resource-exploitation and national demand
which in turn will determine the lines of specialisation of a TPC.

In summary, the TPC is intended to integrate a region's production,
infrastructure, labour and natural resources in a planned,

interdependent and coordinated fashion. By centring on a particular territory, the intention is that economies of scale will logically follow and that with more balanced and planned development between productive and infrastructural activities in particular, living standards will be raised which in turn will contribute to reducing labour turnover.

There are however different types of TPC which can be distinguished on the basis of *scale* and according to a designated region's *level of development*. The first criterion distinguishes between TPCs which are of major national importance and which extend over an entire region. Examples of this type can be found in Fig. 4.3, and include such huge complexes as West Siberia, Kansk-Achinsk, and Saian. These differ from the less ambitious 'nodal' TPCs which are highly localised and are usually based on one large urban-industrial complex.

Although all TPCs are new to the industrial landscape, a further distinction can be drawn between those TPCs which have been consciously created in underdeveloped and sparsely populated regions (*programmo-tselevyye TPK*), primarily in Siberia and the Northlands, and those which have only gradually come to fruition in already industrialised, well-populated areas like European USSR. In the former regions, TPCs are intended to provide the basic form of territorial organisation for a region's development. In the latter, they are primarily intended to make for the more effective management and coordination of already well-established economic activities.

### The TPC as magnet for growth

One measure of the success of the TPC is the extent to which it has succeeded in attracting investment for new industrial projects. Evidence suggests that *Gosplan*, the centralised planning agency responsible for planning the allocation of investments via the economic ministries and departments, is favouring the location of new projects within TPCs. This is notably so in Siberia. Between 70 and 90 percent of all industrial investment earmarked for new construction projects within Siberia is being channelled into these complexes. Moreover, it is particularly the new TPCs, still in the process of formation, where the concentration of funds is greatest. It would seem that TPCs are being used as the basis for a highly selective policy of regional development.

This carries at least one important implication for Siberian development. In earmarking particular regions for the lion's share of new investment, other regions are being neglected. What we are therefore witnessing is the further consolidation of 'two Siberias': one which will form the cornerstone of the region's future, and the other which will remain underpopulated, underfinanced and, in many respects, largely unaltered by the development process. As a consequence, inter-regional disparities within Siberia are likely to grow.

### Departmentalism

We have noted that one of the main aims of the TPC is to eliminate the sectoral barriers that usually describe the organisation of the Soviet economy. There is little evidence to suggest that this goal has been achieved. Indeed, it would seem that the various institutional interests involved in coordinating the TPCs' economic and social activities are not working towards a common goal. Part of the reason for this stems from the limited powers and partisan behaviour of *Gosplan* which, following a 1979 planning decree, was given responsibility for the development of TPCs. *Gosplan* comprises a number of vested interests, including representatives of the major ministries and departments which attempt to get as much out of resource allocation for their particular institution as possible. This 'departmentalism' is further accentuated through the continuing practice of distributing investment funds for construction projects within TPCs through ministerial and departmental channels. The extent of this problem is highlighted by the example of the South Yakutia TPC.

## The South Yakutia TPC

This is one of the newest and largest of Siberia's TPCs and being the most easterly, it has its own special problems. Its major reason for existence is the region's abundance of high-quality coking coal, which is centred around the new town of Neryungri, and is extracted primarily for export. There are also good supplies of other minerals, notably iron ore, and also natural gas. Two ministries have been involved in developing its coal industry: the Coal Ministry and the Ministry of Electric Power. From the outset, however, the Coal Ministry refused to take on the responsibility of providing housing and services to Neryungri's rapidly expanding population. Only those working in the coal industry were to be housed, which meant that the Coal Ministry was only prepared to accommodate two-fifths of the city's 250,000 workforce. Moreover, neither ministry could agree as to where the first house-building programme was to be located, with the Coal Ministry favouring a site near the coalfield and the Ministry of Electric Power a site near a proposed nuclear power plant.

Another common problem is the general lack of responsibility that institutions take for the construction of social infrastructure. The Baykal-Amur Mainline project in South Yakutia highlights this problem. BAM was designed to stimulate the exploitation of hitherto untapped natural resources in its zone of penetration. It was also to provide a supplemental east-west link to the heavily used Trans-Siberian railway. Its construction was plagued by numerous setbacks with its completion in November 1984 well behind schedule. The delays in housing construction and in service provision in particular, were singled out by Soviet commentators as the main reasons for the project's slow progress. In consequence, the scheme found it difficult to attract and retain labour.

## *Perestroika* and the regions

The future development of Siberia will continue to be bound up with the TPC. This was stated at the 27th Party Congress in 1986. Rather than establish more TPCs, the thrust of policy towards the region is to develop existing and already earmarked sites. But Moscow is aware that without resolving inter-sectoral factionalism, little progress will be made. One recent step in overcoming this problem involves a *Gosplan-*

initiated territorial commission, set up to look into the workings of the West Siberia TPC, with the task of improving inter-ministerial and departmental relations. Committees for other TPCs may follow. Representatives of the regions and cities, notably the *soviets*, have also voiced their demands for a further strengthening of their role in territorial planning which Gorbachev's programme of restructuring has encouraged. Indeed the programme of *perestroika* recognises that in order to achieve greater economic efficiency there is a need to give territorial communities more power in the running of their economies, which includes TPCs.

In some respects, however, the laudable aims of *perestroika* do not augur well for Siberia. This is essentially because the priorities singled out to modernise the economy have been linked to maximising returns from investment. As Gorbachev has stated, 'Available investment resources should not be spread around on an even basis. An effort should be made in the new FYP (1986–90) to focus investment on projects that promise the greatest and most immediate return' (*Pravda*, 12 June 1985). Particular sectors and regions of the economy are to benefit. We have already noted that the modernisation of existing plants located primarily in European USSR are to continue to receive priority. The capital investment which will be required to modernise the infrastructure of these existing industries, many built in the 1930s, is considerable. One estimate suggests that it will take ten to fifteen years to overhaul this outmoded industrial infrastructure (*Izvestiya*, 30 June 1986:7).

Industrial modernisation, it is argued, cannot be effectively realised without also transferring basic research into industrial products and applications. Consequently, research and development (R&D) has been singled out for special attention. One of the major problems with R&D at present is that it is organised separately from industrial producers and users of new technology, which has acted as a barrier to innovations finding their way onto the factory floor. Now, ways are being examined to ensure that technological innovations find their way into vital industries. Moreover, R&D is to receive large infusions of capital. This will benefit particularly Moscow and Leningrad – the traditional centres for the diffusion of new technology.

Less finance is to be set aside for the type of large-scale capital-intensive project which has been central to the making of the Siberian economy. The further development of East Siberia is a case in point. The envisaged transformation that the Baykal-Amur Mainline would have had to East Siberia's economy has been revised. No new major resource development projects are envisaged in spite of the mineral wealth of the region opened up by the BAM. Siberia's reputation as the graveyard for investment capital has much to do with such revised strategies. Both high transportation costs combined with the timescale involved in returns on investment continue to work against the region.

# 5 Development, federal colonialism and the non-Russian regions

For most socialist countries, issues of regional development are inextricably bound up with the multiethnic character of society. This is because few socialist countries constitute genuine 'nation-states' in the sense that their territorial boundaries are coextensive with those of a homogenous ethnic community. Consequently, geographically-concentrated ethnic groups vie for a greater share of state resources and for greater control over distribution within their native homelands. Only a handful of socialist countries escape from this dimension to regional development, notably ethnically homogenous Poland, East Germany and Somalia. This leaves a very considerable number with serious ethnoregional divisions in which a dominant nationality must accommodate the regional demands of its ethnic minorities, as in Romania (e.g. Transylvanian Magyars), Bulgaria (e.g. Macedonians), China (e.g. the various non-Han minorities) and in the Soviet Union. In still another group of socialist countries, issues of development and of local control over resources have not always made it possible to contain the competing demands of rival ethnic communities, as in Laos, Yugoslavia, Zimbabwe and Ethiopia, where ethnic divisions at one time or another have erupted into overt violence and even civil war.

## The non-Russian regions: development as stratagem

The Soviet Union is the world's largest multiethinic state. According to the 1979 census, there are 104 ethnic groups (or 'nationalities' in Soviet parlance), the largest grouping being the politically dominant Russians who today constitute just over half of the state population and who are concentrated in the country's historic core territory, the Russian Republic (Fig. 5.1). As part of the socialist federation, the major nationalities have been granted various levels of administrative autonomy for their homelands, the most important of which are the union republics. Together with the Russian Republic, these include the Baltic republics (Estonia, Latvia, Lithuania), the peoples of the western borderlands (Ukraine, Moldavia and Belorussia) and of the Transcaucasus (Azerbaidzhan, Armenia, Georgia), and the predominantly Muslim republics of Central Asia (Kazakhstan, Kirgizia, Turkmenistan, Tadzhikhstan and Uzbekistan).

The state's policy towards its nationalities is viewed as being bound up with the socio-economic development of the non-Russian regions. The least developed republics, notably of Central Asia and Moldavia, are to be brought up to the level of the most advanced by means of industrialisation and urbanisation. Standards of living and the quality of life would thus be improved, which would eventually lead to the

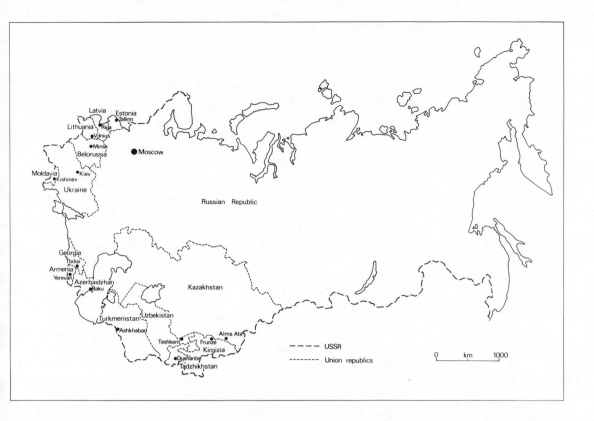

Fig. 5.1 The Soviet Union: the nationality-based union republics.

long-term aim of erasing socio-economic differences between the nationalities. According to recent official pronouncements, the state has met with considerable success in working towards this goal.

It is also argued that important consequences follow from regional transformation in terms of the way in which the nationalities relate to their multinational state. In essence, socio-economic development is envisaged as weakening parochially-based ethnic identities in favour of a consciousness of being part of the values and culture of one Soviet people (*Sovetskii narod*). That a degree of cultural assimilation has occurred should not be underestimated; a strong sense of patriotism and of shared socialist values does transcend nationality boundaries. But equally, it is also evident that socio-economic development has not had the transformative impact in weakening local national loyalties that was envisaged. As First Party Secretary, Mikhail Gorbachev, now acknowledges, 'Regrettably, we used to stress our really considerable achievements in the solution of the nationality problem and assessed the situation in high flow terms. But this is real life with all its diversity and all its difficulties' (1987:118–19). In the non-Russian republics, nationalism is indeed far from being a spent force. Since the mid-1980s in particular, there has been a major resurgence in nationality demands throughout all the non-Russian union republics, particularly in Central Asia, the Transcaucasus and in the Baltic. Much of this resurgence is tied in with issues of regional development and of the right of nationalities to have more say in the way in which their homelands are organised and their economies managed. Thus the multiethnic character of the Soviet Union adds another important dimension to understanding why issues of development are of political significance.

## Federal colonialism

When it comes to the way in which the Soviet state treats the development of its non-Russian regions, it is often contended that it can best be summed up in terms of a particular variant of a dominance-dependency relationship; that of a politically dominant Russian state exploiting its non-Russian periphery as a colonial power would its colonies. Rather than ending the exploitative nature of ethnic relations characteristic of its colonial predecessor, the territorially expansionist tsarist Empire, the Soviet state continues to maintain a colonial relationship with its non-Russian regions, based on economic exploitation and on social injustice. It is considered a form of internal colonialism in which Russia proper benefits by keeping the non-Russian regions underdeveloped and powerless.

Such a model of dominance-dependency has been sketched out by Wallerstein (1973) in relation to Soviet Central Asia. He suggests that there are four features which characterise these non-Russian republics. In summary, they are as follows:

1   *Limited degree of political autonomy*   The regions are denied any self-government in a state where power is highly centralised and where the major decisions which affect the lives of the regions are made in Moscow.
2   *Narrow range of economic activities*   The economies of the regions remain highly specialised and so dependent on a more diversified Russian core territory. In remaining a predominantly agrarian and underdeveloped economy, Central Asia provides a necessary source of agricultural produce and raw materials for the benefit of Russia proper.
3   *Limited social stratification*   As a consequence of Central Asia being designated an agrarian economy, its native population are concentrated in agriculture and suffer from all the problems associated with underdevelopment. The native population therefore remain less equipped to enter the urban arena of skilled employment; they are thus under-represented in the region's more specialist and managerial occupations which tend to be filled by incoming Russians.
4   *Lower standard of living*   Due to the region's underdevelopment, Central Asia has a poorer standard of living and quality of life than that of Russia proper.

So as a consequence of both ethnic and regional discrimination, Central Asia earns the title of 'an internal colony' and its peoples that of a subjugated minority. Of course, it is important to distinguish between underdeveloped Central Asia and the fully industrialised European non-Russian republics of the Ukraine, Belorussia and the Baltic. As union republics, they all possess limited territorial powers. All also possess a highly specialised core-dependent economy, but in the case of the European non-Russian republics, it is based on over-specialised sectors of modern industry. However, unlike Central Asia, native urbanisation in the European non-Russian republics has resulted in a greater diversity of social structure, with the indigenous population being well represented in the urban-based professions and in the political and administrative life of their republics. Concomitant with this social diversity is a native standard of living comparable to if not often higher than that of the Russian Republic. Does this therefore mean that we can talk of a colonial relationship only with regard to Central Asia? What would seem more applicable is to examine how these differences between core and periphery have come about and whether development policy discriminates against particular non-Russian regions.

The state's near territorial monopoly over investment allocation provides it with the facility to engineer 'development' in favour of its own self-sustaining interests. In this respect, two interests dominated the early years of industrialisation: economic growth and geo-strategic considerations. The former tended to favour those regions where investment was likely to register the greatest return. Thus during the period of the country's industrialisation, it was particularly the Russian republic (including resource-rich Siberia) and the Ukraine which received the bulk of investment. Secondly, geo-strategic considerations dictated the location of industry away from the ethnic borderlands and into the defensible regions of the Russian interior. So the initial process of uneven development was based not on 'ethnic considerations' but rather on the facts of economic growth and defence. Considerations of ethnic equalisation during the industrialisation drive and immediately after took a definite second place. We get some indication of the impact of such policies of differential development by comparing the level of urbanisation of the Central Asian republics with that of Russia proper (Table 5.1). As an indicator of economic development, the level

**Table 5.1   Indices of socio-economic development for the union republics, 1940–87**

| | Population (millions) | Urbanisation % of total population | | Industrial growth | Students in higher education per 10,000 population | | Doctors per 10,000 population | |
|---|---|---|---|---|---|---|---|---|
| | 1987 | 1940 | 1987 | 1986 (1940=1) | 1940/41 | 1986/87 | 1940 | 1986 |
| USSR | 281.7 | 33 | 66 | 26 | 41 | 181 | 7.9 | 42.7 |
| Russian republic | 145.3 | 34 | 74 | 23 | 43 | 200 | 8.2 | 45.7 |
| Ukraine | 51.2 | 34 | 67 | 18 | 47 | 166 | 8.4 | 41.9 |
| Belorussia | 10.0 | 21 | 64 | 40 | 24 | 179 | 5.7 | 38.3 |
| Moldavia | 4.2 | 13 | 47 | 69 | 10 | 126 | 4.2 | 38.4 |
| Estonia | 1.6 | 34 | 72 | 58 | | | 10.0 | 47.3 |
| Latvia | 2.7 | 35 | 71 | 55 | 52 | 164 | 13.2 | 48.8 |
| Lithuania | 3.6 | 23 | 67 | 77 | 20 | 178 | 6.7 | 43.6 |
| Armenia | 3.4 | 28 | 68 | 64 | 82 | 160 | 7.5 | 38.6 |
| Azerbaidzhan | 6.8 | 37 | 54 | 17 | 44 | 155 | 10.0 | 38.4 |
| Georgia | 5.3 | 31 | 55 | 22 | 77 | 163 | 13.3 | 55.4 |
| Kazakhstan | 16.2 | 30 | 58 | 40 | 16 | 169 | 4.3 | 38.1 |
| Turkmenistan | 3.4 | 35 | 48 | 14 | 22 | 117 | 7.6 | 33.8 |
| Tadzhikhstan | 4.8 | 19 | 33 | 22 | 15 | 115 | 4.1 | 26.9 |
| Kirghizia | 4.1 | 22 | 40 | 49 | 19 | 141 | 3.8 | 34.2 |
| Uzbekistan | 19.0 | 25 | 42 | 22 | 28 | 153 | 4.7 | 34.1 |

*Source:* Gosudarstvennyi komitet SSSR po statistike (1987) *Narodnoe Khozyaistvo SSSR za 70 let,* Moscow, Finansy i Statistika, pp. 20, 132, 374, 378–9, 550

of urbanisation of Russia proper is not only far higher than that of Central Asia but it also occurred at a far faster rate.

Yet what is equally as significant is that urbanisation has occurred at a relatively rapid rate in all the Central Asian republics. The industrialisation of these republics, particularly since the mid-1950s, has been considerable. While most industrial activity tends to be geared towards the region's rural economy (e.g. food processing, textile industries, processing of minerals), there is also a significant heavy engineering and iron and steel industry, particularly in Kazakhstan, the most industrialised of the Central Asian republics. A substantial flow of capital, from Russia proper and from the other more industrialised republics, has thus gone into financing Central Asia's industrialisation. It is on such a scale that if market forces had been the only determinant of capital investment, Central Asia would have been neglected.

Nor has Central Asia's social development been forgotten. Illiteracy was commonplace before the establishment of Soviet power. In 1926, between 3.8 percent (Tadzhikstan) and 16.5 percent (Kirgizia) of the population were literate; by the end of the 1950s, literacy was more or less universal. As Table 5.1 shows, considerable improvements have also occurred in the arena of medical provision and education. In general, while the standard of living of Central Asians still lags behind most other republics, as also reflected in their rates of urbanisation (we have noted that urbanites enjoy appreciably higher living standards and better access to services and amenities), the level of social well-being has improved immeasurably over the past few decades. Indeed, it has been shown that when compared with other Muslim countries, Soviet Central Asia enjoys a higher per caput income and is better provided for in more or less all aspects of living standards. Small wonder then that Moscow holds up Central Asia as a model for third-world development. Moreover, there is no evidence to suggest that Moscow purposely discriminates against Central Asians in terms of income, housing or jobs.

With regard to overall investment since the early 1960s, however, differences do persist between the republics due primarily to reasons of economic return, but these trends cannot be understood in simple core-periphery terms (Table 5.2). The gap in inter-regional dispersion of

**Table 5.2 Regional shares of Soviet investment, 1946–84 (percentage figures)**

|  | Russian Republic | Ukraine | Belorussia and Moldavia | Baltic | Trans-caucasus | Central Asia |
|---|---|---|---|---|---|---|
| 1946–50 | 61.23 | 19.35 | 3.36 | 1.29 | 5.27 | 8.64 |
| 1951–55 | 64.25 | 16.52 | 2.83 | 1.33 | 4.70 | 9.46 |
| 1956–60 | 63.37 | 16.98 | 3.03 | 1.44 | 3.49 | 10.99 |
| 1961–65 | 62.39 | 17.63 | 3.70 | 1.90 | 3.77 | 13.39 |
| 1966–70 | 58.92 | 16.49 | 4.19 | 2.04 | 3.82 | 13.39 |
| 1971–75 | 60.26 | 15.93 | 4.51 | 3.11 | 3.45 | 12.68 |
| 1976–80 | 61.90 | 14.78 | 4.48 | 2.85 | 2.89* | 12.34 |
| 1981–84 | 62.25 | 13.84 | 4.46 | 2.84 | 3.96 | 12.50 |

* excludes Armenia

*Source:* Calculated by D. Bahry (1987) *Outside Moscow. Power, politics and budgetary policy in the Soviet republics*, Columbia University Press, New York, p. 116.

investment narrowed during the 1960s, widened slightly in the mid-1970s, and then levelled off. While the overall trend has been one of convergence, some republics have benefited more than others, notably Central Asia, the Baltic and Belorussia/Moldavia. In contrast, total USSR investment in the Russian Republic and the Ukraine has been downward as the emphasis on investing in the traditional manufacturing sector has lessened.

In the sphere of social welfare, where the state has been most effective in implementing ethnoregional equalisation, there is every indication to suggest that a considerable transfer of wealth has occurred from the relatively rich to the relatively poor republics. In one study of regional budgetary policy, Zwick (1979) came to the conclusion that ethnoregional differences were becoming more rather than less marked, suggesting little commitment by Moscow to eradicating differences in standards of living, particularly between Central Asia and the other republics. Closer examination of his findings, however, show that it was not a question of the state's lack of commitment to Central Asia's development, but rather that budgetary allocation had failed to keep pace with the faster demographic growth of the region. In practice, there is a considerable transfer of wealth to Central Asia; the problem is that its actual impact over time is limited by its fewer resources (e.g. skilled labour, raw materials, access to markets) *vis-à-vis* other mechanisms of resource allocation (i.e. the industrial ministries).

One of the clearest indicators of social development is the degree to which the proportion of each nationality has a higher education. If we compare the educational attainment of native Central Asians with that of Russians (where the Russians = 100), we find that the late-modernising Central Asians have made considerable improvement over recent decades. In the 1959–70 period, the relative score of Uzbeks increased from 36 to 53, that of Tadzhiks from 32 to 47, and Kazakhs from 44 to 64 (Jones and Grupp, 1984). A growing native middle class has therefore emerged in the region and reflects a degree of social convergence between the Central Asian and Russian nationalities.

State affirmative action policies towards natives in the non-Russian republics have also speeded up the process by which individuals can climb the social ladder. Within their regions, natives receive preferential treatment in relation to entrance into higher education, particular employment, and party membership, all of which have facilitated the employment of Central Asians in administration, economic management and in the professions. This has one important implication in particular for the politics of development. In contrast to key positions in party, government and administration in Moscow where Russians are over-represented, natives are generally well represented in such posts in their union republics. There is of course considerable variation from union republic to union republic, ranging from the Transcaucasus where the indigenous nationalities are over-represented in proportion to their number, to Central Asia and Moldavia where natives are less well represented. The important point is that when it comes to issues of resource allocation, such questions are more likely to be bound up with ethnic politics as native leaders attempt to secure from a Russian-dominated centre the best possible outcome for their nationality-republic.

It would therefore seem that the 'internal colonial' thesis has limited applicability. Instead the label 'federal colonialism' might be more useful. This notion reflects the essential contradiction in policy by the state towards the non-Russian regions. On the one hand, particularly into modern times, the state has purposely pursued a policy of regional equalisation, specifically in relation to social welfare and improving native standards of living. Union republic status also ensures native access to upward mobility as well as the preservation of their languages and cultures. On the other hand, the state continues to pursue a form of colonialism in a political sense, ensuring that power remains highly centralised and that federalism, at least in the Western sense, remains a façade. It also curtails native cultural and political activities whenever state security in the regions is in question.

## Developmental issues: the Baltic republics

Issues of resource allocation dominate much of the agenda of federal politics. While the centralised nature of allocative decision-making does limit the impact that the regions have in directly influencing and successfully negotiating their spatial allocation, none the less nowadays they are far from being impotent. In their negotiations with the centre, regional leaders have adopted a number of tactics in order to promote local development. Couching demands as being in 'the national interest' is one notable practice. Recently, the Ukrainian First Party Secretary has argued that revitalising the Donbass' traditional manufacturing base will stimulate overall economic growth, while his counterpart in Tadzhikhstan argues that given the problems that industry in European USSR is having with labour shortages, it is in the common interest to develop the industrial base of his republic where labour resources are plentiful. Often the outcome of such negotiations is a compromise. For instance, recently Lithuania requested 44 million rubles from the Ministry of the Chemical Industry to increase synthetic fibre and chemical fertiliser production and to open a new plastics plant: the Ministry handed over 5 million rubles (Bahry, 1987:89). In their lobbying efforts, regions clearly have different agendas, in part determined by the priorities of the regional authorities, and set by local conditions. One of the most vocal regions in this regard is that of the Baltic republics.

The small Baltic republics of Estonia, Latvia and Lithuania occupy a unique position in the Soviet federal structure. They only became part of the Soviet Union during the Second World War when each was forced to give up a shortlived but formative period of interwar independent statehood (1918–40). Then, not only did the Baltic peoples experience managing their own economic affairs, but they did so relatively successfully. Their pre-Soviet economies were based largely on a highly efficient agricultural sector and upon a well-educated and skilled labour force. Loss of sovereignty, however, resulted in power being transferred to Moscow. In the case of Estonia and Latvia, it also resulted in their rapid industrialisation. Due probably to its less developed industrial base, Lithuania's industrial development was delayed until much later. It was, however, particularly the character and speed of forced industrialisation which was of concern in Estonia and Latvia. First, industrialisation meant the development of heavy industry at the expense of both agriculture and light manufacturing industry. This occurred despite the lack of local raw materials and energy supplies to support economic restructuring. From a purely economic standpoint, the development of a heavy industrial base did not seem to make sense. Recently, however, more concern has been paid to building up those sectors more in keeping with local resources (e.g. agriculture) and skills (e.g. high technology), although about a third of the republics' industrial workforce is still employed in heavy engineering. The second concern was over the speed of industrialisation. The rapid growth of metallurgical and machine-building plants was such that a large additional labour force was required, for the demands of heavy industry soon outstripped the indigenous labour supply. Yet both Estonia and Latvia already had one of the lowest birth rates in Europe, a trend which has continued into modern times. In 1987, for example, natural population increase for both republics stood at 4.0 per thousand population, the lowest recorded in the Soviet Union, and at a level in which the native population can barely reproduce itself. In short, industrialisation has meant that supplementary labour has had to be brought in from other republics, primarily from Russia. As Table 5.3 shows, this inter-republic migration, principally into the cities, continues. In Latvia it now accounts for just under two-thirds of the republic's population growth. This contrasts with Lithuania which in having a higher birth rate and having avoided rapid industrialisation, has not needed to recruit a large labour force from elsewhere.

It is therefore not surprising that the twin issues of regional management and the direction of the Baltic economy should dominate much of the local political agenda. There is considerable support in the region for greater territorial autonomy over the running of the republics' economies and for slowing down growth rates in all industries not producing for the local population. The Baltic republics therefore welcomed the decision in the late 1950s to devolve economic powers from the centrally organised industrial ministries to the regions. This involved the setting up of 105 countrywide regional economic councils (or *sovnarkhozy*), which included one for each of the Baltic republics. As a result of this decision, regional interests flourished, often at the expense of All-Union interests. This was partly a

**Table 5.3 Net migration into the Latvian republic, 1951–84**

|  | Population growth | Natural increase | | Net migration | |
|---|---|---|---|---|---|
|  | thousands | thousands | % | thousands | % |
| 1951–55 | 66.4 | 49.5 | 74 | 16.9 | 26 |
| 1956–60 | 123.7 | 65.7 | 53 | 58.0 | 47 |
| 1961–65 | 135.2 | 57.1 | 42 | 78.1 | 58 |
| 1966–70 | 107.2 | 38.6 | 36 | 68.5 | 64 |
| 1971–75 | 110.3 | 34.2 | 31 | 76.1 | 69 |
| 1979–84 | 66.0 | 25.0 | 38 | 41.0 | 62 |

*Sources:* Ya. Ya. Rudzat and E. K. Vitolins (1977) 'Latviiskaya Sovetskaya Sotsialisticheskaya Respublika', in T. V. Ryabushkin (ed.) *Naselenie Soyuznykh Respublik*, Moscow, p. 209. Data for 1979–84 calculated from *Narodnoe Khozyaistvo SSSR*, 1979 to 1984.

consequence of the nature of the *sovnarkhoz* system in which due to the lack of coordination and communication between *sovnarkhozy*, regions tended to plan, manage and divert investment funds under their control to local needs, often at the expense of other regions. But it was also a consequence of what Moscow was later to condemn as 'national narrow-mindedness' in which local leaders were criticised for purposely putting the interests of their nationality-republic before those of the country. In Latvia, for instance, a considerable effort was made to re-orient its economy away from heavy industry and further rapid industrialisation, towards developing those sectors of the economy – like craft industries, agriculture and light manufacturing – which were more characteristic of the Latvian economy during its years as an independent state. Such policies also had the temporary effect of reducing what many in the republic saw as the undesirable flow of Russians into the region. In its concern over the way in which the regions were managing their economic affairs, Moscow abolished the *sovnarkhozy*. By the early 1960s, power had been restored to the centre and to the industrial ministries.

The failure of the centralised ministries to allocate sufficient funds to regional industries and to effect such allocations by taking into account the particular needs of the region remains a major area of tension. The cause of this is interpreted as lying with the widespread ministerial practice of departmentalism (which we discussed in the last chapter), in which the ministries have shown themselves to be largely insensitive to the regions and to their local needs. Another issue to surface concerns the insensitive way in which preoccupation with industrial development has resulted in the mismanagement and depletion of local natural resources, notably the region's forests and the oil shale reserves of northern Estonia. Locally, much is also made of the need to protect the environment, especially from water pollution generated by the introduction of large-scale industrial plants.

It is however the pressing problem of labour shortages which has been the focus of most local attention. Many of the republics' economists and planners see the solution to this problem in switching to a more intensive course of development. Here the emphasis is on securing economic growth through improving labour efficiency and productivity rather than by further increases in labour migration. Emphasis on the modernisation of existing plants and on the further development of already well-established capital-intensive, high-technology industries, is advocated. But such ways of restructuring and improving the region's economies are also seen as bound up with the need for more regional planning and for greater power for the regions in the management of regional development.

Finally, there is also the thorny issue of the economic contribution of the Baltic republics to the state budget. As one of the most productive economies, there is resentment that wealth generated in the region is being used to finance the economic and social development of other regions. This, it is suggested, is particularly unfair given that local capital could be used to improve the republics' increasingly stretched urban services and amenities (*Pravda*, 9 February 1988).

Viewed in relation to other regions, the Baltic republics enjoy considerable economic prosperity and a standard of living for its peoples comparable to none. Yet for historic reasons, the comparisons that the Balts make with regard to their levels of socio-economic development tend to be with the more prosperous and sovereign states of neighbouring Scandinavia and Eastern Europe. They also tend to evaluate their own circumstances in relation to an idealised past, particularly the interwar years. Such comparisons fuel further demands for more resources and for greater say in the running of their own affairs.

## Russian immigration, job competition and the threat to national cultures

One of the major ethnic and demographic consequences of economic development for all the non-Russian regions has been immigration, principally from the Russian Republic. Today just under a quarter of all Russians live in the non-Russian republics, a sizeable proportion of whom have migrated from their homeland in the Soviet period Table 5.4).

It is a migration which has generally followed the contours of industrialisation and the resulting demand for supplemental labour in the non-Russian regions. Principal recipients of this migration have been the eastern Ukraine, Central Asia (particularly Kazakhstan), and the Baltic republics. It is a migration which is also urban in destination, primarily into the major cities. Such is its scale that in a number of the republics' capital cities, the Russians constitute the largest community (e.g. Riga, Alma Ata, Frunze). The only republics to escape from large-scale in-migration have been the two

**Table 5.4   Nationality composition of the union republics, 1959 and 1979**

|                  | Population (millions) | | Native nationality (%) | | Russians (%) | |
|------------------|------|------|------|------|------|------|
|                  | 1959 | 1979 | 1959 | 1979 | 1959 | 1979 |
| Russian republic | 117.5 | 137.5 | 83.3 | 82.6 | —  | —  |
| Ukraine          | 41.9 | 49.8 | 76.8 | 73.6 | 16.3 | 21.1 |
| Belorussia       | 8.0  | 9.5  | 81.1 | 79.4 | 8.2  | 11.9 |
| Moldavia         | 2.9  | 3.9  | 65.4 | 63.9 | 10.2 | 12.8 |
| Estonia          | 1.2  | 1.5  | 74.6 | 64.7 | 20.1 | 27.9 |
| Latvia           | 2.0  | 2.5  | 62.0 | 53.7 | 26.6 | 32.8 |
| Lithuania        | 2.7  | 3.4  | 79.3 | 80.0 | 8.5  | 8.9  |
| Georgia          | 4.0  | 5.0  | 64.3 | 68.8 | 10.1 | 7.4  |
| Armenia          | 1.8  | 3.0  | 88.0 | 89.7 | 3.2  | 2.3  |
| Azerbaidzhan     | 3.7  | 6.0  | 67.5 | 78.1 | 13.6 | 7.9  |
| Turkmenistan     | 1.5  | 2.8  | 60.9 | 68.4 | 17.3 | 12.6 |
| Uzbekistan       | 8.3  | 15.4 | 61.1 | 68.7 | 13.5 | 10.8 |
| Tadzhikhstan     | 2.0  | 3.8  | 53.1 | 58.8 | 13.3 | 10.4 |
| Kirghizia        | 2.0  | 3.5  | 40.0 | 47.9 | 30.2 | 25.9 |
| Kazakhstan       | 9.1  | 14.7 | 30.0 | 36.0 | 42.7 | 40.8 |

*Source:* Tsentral'noe Statisticheskoe Upravlenie SSSR (1980) *Naselenie SSSR. Po dannym vsesoyoznoi perepisi naseleniya 1979 goda*, Izdatel'stvo politicheskoi literatury, Moscow, pp. 27–30.

Transcaucasian republics of Armenia and Georgia. Although these republics enjoy a high standard of living, lack of an energy base and distance from European markets have resulted in a more limited industrial sector. Local industrial needs have also been more than adequately met by a highly skilled native workforce.

This 'intermingling of national cultures' is officially viewed as a positive phenomenon and an important ingredient of nationalities policy. But the problem is that such a policy relies mainly on the mobility of the Russian population. Many Western writers interpret such migration as designed to ensure the cultural assimilation of non-Russians into a Russian-dominated state. Along with centrally planned industrialisation, Russian migration is viewed as a synonym for the Russification of the non-Russian regions. Yet there is little evidence to suggest that this has occurred on any sizeable scale. If we take languages spoken as a crude indicator of degree of cultural assimilation, then as Table 5.5 shows, although a small proportion of each nationality declare Russian as their first language, in the 1959–79 intercensal period, the proportion of each nationality declaring their namesake nationality language as their native language remained high and relatively static. Only the Belorussians and Ukrainians, who like the Russians are Slavs, and who traditionally have had a high proportion of Russian speakers, have high levels of linguistic assimilation (89.1 and 83.5 percent respectively). More significant, however, is the adoption of Russian as a second language. Especially over the past two decades, native bilingualism has increased but it is highly uneven. It is particularly high in the more industrialised

**Table 5.5  The non-Russian nationalities: languages spoken, 1959–79**

| Nationality within homeland | Percentage regarding this nationality language as their native tongue | | | Percentage claiming good knowledge of Russian as second language[b] | | |
|---|---|---|---|---|---|---|
| | 1959 | 1979 | Change[a] | 1970 | 1979 | Change[a] |
| Ukrainians | 93.5 | 89.1 | −4.4 | 28.6 | 51.7 | 23.1 |
| Belorussians | 93.2 | 83.5 | −9.7 | 52.5 | 62.9 | 10.4 |
| Moldavians | 98.2 | 96.5 | −1.7 | 33.9 | 46.2 | 6.3 |
| Estonians | 99.3 | 99.0 | −0.3 | 27.6 | 23.1 | −4.5 |
| Latvians | 98.4 | 97.8 | −0.6 | 45.3 | 58.3 | 13.0 |
| Lithuanians | 99.2 | 99.7 | 0.5 | 34.8 | 52.2 | 17.4 |
| Armenians | 99.2 | 99.4 | 0.2 | 23.2 | 34.2 | 11.0 |
| Azerbaidzhanis | 98.1 | 98.7 | 0.6 | 14.9 | 27.9 | 13.0 |
| Georgians | 99.5 | 99.2 | −0.3 | 20.1 | 25.5 | 5.4 |
| Tadzhikhs | 99.3 | 99.3 | 0.0 | 16.6 | 27.8 | 11.2 |
| Uzbeks | 98.6 | 98.8 | 0.2 | 13.0 | 52.9 | 39.9 |
| Turkmens | 99.5 | 99.2 | −0.3 | 14.8 | 24.2 | 9.4 |
| Kirghiz | 99.7 | 99.6 | −0.1 | 19.8 | 28.5 | 8.7 |
| Kazakhs | 99.2 | 98.6 | −0.6 | 41.8 | 50.6 | 8.8 |

[a] change is the percentage point change between the two dates
[b] the 1959 census did not include a question on knowledge of Russian as a second language
*Sources:* Tsentral'noe Statistcheskoe Upravelenie pri Sovete Ministrov SSR, 1962; 1972–73.
*Vestnik Statistiki*, 1980, 7, p. 43; 1980, 8, pp. 64–70; 1980, 9, pp. 61–70; 1980, 10, pp. 67–73; 1980, 11, pp. 60–4.

republics, like the Baltic and the Ukraine, and is also pri.. feature of the cities. There are good reasons why this is the the more advanced the society, the greater the pressure to c in the official language of the state. Nowadays one needs Rus an urban professional but not to operate a combine harvester collective farm. Second, the pressure to communicate in the stat language is far greater in the cities not only because a sizeable proportion of the population is Russian but also because it is necessary to use the Russian language in the professions and in more specialised employment. There are several implications of the spread of Russian for both native employment and for survival of national cultures.

First, there is the question of whether a knowledge of Russian is a precondition to native social and economic advancement. The native languages enjoy a privileged position within their namesake republics; education is available in the native language and it is these schools that natives opt to attend. Indeed, much of public life is oriented around the native language: the media, administration, and local party life. Yet the pressure to learn Russian comes from two quarters: first, it is a precondition to entrance into higher education, itself an important stepping-stone to professional employment; second, due to the Russian language being singled out as the official language of the state, there is little pressure on Russians living in the non-Russian republics to learn the native language (and few bother to do so). As the experience of Central Asians shows, lack of knowledge of Russian inhibits career mobility. In the Central Asian countryside, where the majority of natives predominate, schools are generally poorer than elsewhere, as are the facilities for the teaching of the Russian language. This is one

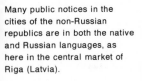
Many public notices in the cities of the non-Russian republics are in both the native and Russian languages, as here in the central market of Riga (Latvia).

important reason why Central Asia displays the lowest knowledge of Russian of any republic. Escaping from the countryside to work on the factory floor does not demand a knowledge of Russian, but entrance into higher education and to an eventual middle-class employment does. Thus Central Asians have to compete in their own cities for the best jobs with individuals for whom Russian is the native language. There is therefore much resentment among the native population at the way in which Russian migrants have filled many of the more lucrative positions in economic management and in administration which they feel should naturally be theirs.

The second issue concerns whether the spread of Russian poses a threat to the survival of national cultures. Ironically, in the less developed republics, it could be argued that the slower pace of indigenous development has helped to protect native cultures. In the more industrialised republics, like the Baltic for example, the fear is that the spread of Russian could undermine the continuation of the indigenous language and culture. According to one leading Estonian scholar, 'the logical process of the internationalisation of culture and the intermingling among the population is often resented by part of the population'. One main reason for this, he argues, is that there is 'a disdainful attitude by the non-indigenous population [in the republic] towards the Estonian language and the culture of the republic's native population' (*Pravda*, 9 February 1988). Resentment at having to learn Russian, combined with the fear that its spread could jeopardise the future of the native language and culture, continues to fuel ethnic discontent.

### Development as a resource for stability

Centrally directed resource allocation remains a powerful political weapon in furnishing ethnic stability in the non-Russian regions. Where improvements in standards of living or economic investment fall short of local expectations, then discontent does arise. So far, political manifestations of such discontent have been largely confined to the formal arena of centre-union republic politics in which native leaders argue the case for more resources and for particular developmental projects for their regions. But such issues have also helped to fuel recent nationalist demonstrations and riots in Kazakhstan (1986), Transcaucasia (1988) and in the Baltic republics (1987–88). Moreover, there has been a notable increase in demands for greater local say in how resources should be allocated, managed and planned, to which Moscow is now more sympathetic. The union republics have been given greater responsibility in providing consumer services and there are also plans to expand their managerial role in other spheres as well (*Pravda*, 26 February 1986). Yet until much of the power of the industrial ministries is devolved to the regions, such reforms are likely to fall short of local demands.

With regard to how future resources are to be allocated, important decisions need to be made. Nowhere is this more the case than in the Baltic republics and Central Asia. In the former, capital is needed in order to facilitate the economy's intensification (which would mean less reliance on outside labour) and the more effective utilisation of local resources. In spite of the region's relative social prosperity, a growing concern about living standards and the need to spend more on urban services and housing is also apparent. In Central Asia, the major issues are to do with the increasing economic and social demands of a rapidly growing population. More industrial development is required in order to absorb the region's growing labour surplus. But in its concern with overall economic growth, the state has so far shown itself unprepared to make a significant shift in investment resources from the North to the South. In terms of regional welfare provision, a sizeable increase in state resources will also be required if Moscow is to sustain, let alone improve, Central Asian living standards. In such regions then, questions of development become bound up with ethnic politics. It is the price the Soviet Union has to pay for its multiethnic character.

# 6 Rural development

Within the agenda of territorial priorities set by the state, the countryside now occupies a more prominent position. Stalin's strategy of combined and uneven development, which starved rural areas of much-needed capital investment, has been superseded by policies which single out the countryside for special treatment. There are a number of reasons for this marked shift in attitude. First, it is acknowledged that an undercapitalised and inefficient rural economy acts as a major brake on the economic and social prosperity of a rapidly growing urban population (which increased fourfold in the 1959–87 period), and on national economic growth more generally. The importance of food as a social resource is also linked to the second reason for concern about the countryside. Soviet leaders are only too well aware – as recent events in troubled Poland show – that an improved and more varied diet provided at an affordable price is bound up with maintaining political and social stability. Last, it is acknowledged that if erasing differences in the standard of living between town and countryside is to be realised, then the state must direct more of its energies towards improving the quality of life in rural areas.

In spite of the countryside now being a net recipient of substantial resources in terms of capital investment and subsidies, agriculture still remains the weak spot of the national economy. The state continues to be dependent on a Western-dominated world economy in order to meet such shortfalls in products. Due to a series of poor harvests from 1979 into the mid-1980s, the Soviet Union found it necessary to import an average of 30 million metric tonnes of grain per year between 1981 and 1984, much of it from the United States and other Western countries. Besides making the USSR more susceptible to the unpredictability of

**Table 6.1  Population growth and rural change, 1913–80**

|  | 1913 | 1926 | 1939 | 1971 | 1980 |
|---|---|---|---|---|---|
| Area sown (millions of hectares) | 105 | 112 | 138 | 207 | 217 |
| Fallow land (as % of land under cultivation) | 30 | — | 13 | 8 | 6 |
| Average wheat yields (quintals per ha) | 7.3 | — | — | 12.5 | 14 |
| Total population (millions) | 139 | 147 | 170 | 244 | 266 |
| Active farming populations (millions) | 65 | 68.5 | 35–40 | 30–35 | 27 |
| Number of mouths fed by a single farmer | 2.15 | 2.15 | 4.5 | 7.5 | 9.8 |
| Area of land under cultivation per inhabitant (ha) | 0.76 | 0.76 | 0.81 | 0.85 | 0.81 |

*Source:* B. Kerblay (1983) *Modern Soviet Society*, Methuen, London, p. 28.

global politics, becoming a net importer of grain also means that valuable foreign currency raised by exporting oil, cannot be spent on much-needed Western high technology. Given, then, that low agricultural productivity carries implications for the whole of the economy, it is not surprising that successive leaders since Stalin have ranked it high on their list of priorities. For Gorbachev, this means making substantial changes to the way in which the rural economy is organised in order to fulfil the set goal of making the Soviet Union self-sufficient in agricultural produce and foodstuffs in the shortest time possible.

This chapter begins by examining the development strategies that successive leaders since Stalin have adopted in order to improve agricultural productivity. We then explore changes to the organisation of rural production, paying particular attention to the conflicts of interest that exist between the local party, collective farm managers and the peasantry in the production process. The chapter is rounded off by examining recent attempts to improve the social well-being of the countryside. (See Table 6.1.)

## Rural development strategies

By the end of the 1950s, the Soviet Union had joined other developed countries in reaching its limit to the extensive development of agriculture. Khrushchev's Virgin Lands campaign of the mid-1950s, which brought the marginal and semi-arid lands of Northern Kazakhstan and South-West Siberia (Tselinnyi *kray*) under the plough, was the last major attempt to increase agricultural output by extending the area of cultivated land. Extensification has been replaced by intensification as the basis for development. In order to ensure higher agricultural production and a simultaneous increase in the productivity of rural labour, the emphasis has been on vast investments in artificial fertilisers, soil improvement, mechanisation, irrigation and rural infrastructure. It would, however, be wrong to interpret such a switch in strategy as based on no risk-taking. True, Soviet leaders since Khrushchev have certainly learned from the problems associated with a highly controversial Virgin Lands Programme, which by 1960 had brought 42 million hectares under seed, representing some 20 percent of the country's sown area in that year. The notion that overall agricultural productivity can be raised overnight from minimal investment in high-risk, grandiose projects has been abandoned. The consequences this strategy had in reducing soil fertility, eventually leading to the disastrous crop failure of 1963, are only too fresh in the memory of today's decision-takers. Greater emphasis is now put on investing in European USSR, such as in the rich chernozem region of the Ukraine, where agricultural performance is less sensitive to the capriciousness of weather conditions. Yet while subsequent leaders have been more concerned with taking fewer risks and acknowledge that return on investment will not reap benefits overnight, none the less experimentation and costly capital-intensive projects remain based on the ethos that desperate problems require radical solutions.

Depending on the regional context, there are a number of strategies which can be adopted in order to improve agricultural production through intensification. They involve capital being invested in particular forms of technology geared towards mechanisation, land drainage, irrigation schemes, artificial fertilisers, roads, and the like. Yet such strategies of agricultural modernisation envisage different ways in which traditional inputs into the production process – namely land and labour – can be augmented or replaced through intensification. It can involve technology replacing farm labour in areas where there are labour shortages and where the land/labour ratio is relatively high. The strategy is labour saving and output per worker rises. This sort of strategy has been applied to many parts of European USSR. An alternative strategy involves technology being used to increase the agricultural area, most appropriately where the land/labour ratio is low. It is land saving and output per hectare rises. This strategy has been applied to many southern regions of the USSR. In short, investment has been geared towards those regional resources which are most scarce, namely labour in the north and land in the south. The following two case studies illustrate the way in which two large-scale development projects attempt to resolve the problems associated with low agricultural productivity in the north and the south. Besides illustrating the problems associated with each strategy, these projects also highlight the role that vested interest groups play in questions of rural development and the various arguments that are put forward as to how best capital can be used in order to raise agricultural productivity.

### The Central Non-Black Earth Zone (CNBEZ)

Successive Party Congresses since 1974 have singled out the Central Non-Black Earth Zone of European USSR (CNBEZ) for particular treatment. Since the establishment of this programme, some 31.2 billion rubles of capital investments have been ploughed into a region stretching from Leningrad to the Urals, and which takes in the most urbanised part of the USSR, including the Moscow conurbation (Fig. 6.1). It is a region of mixed farming, embracing such crops as rye, oats, wheat, potatoes and flax, with market gardening and dairying also important. Most of the capital invested has been earmarked for deliveries of mineral fertiliser, improving and expanding the rural infrastructure, and in drainage projects. In short, the aim of the CNBEZ programme is to revive the region's traditionally important contribution to agriculture which, primarily as a result of rural depopulation and limited capital investment in agricultural mechanisation and rural infrastructure, had declined considerably. Yet is was also acknowledged that the podzolic soils of the region could never provide the high returns from capital input on the scale of the rich chernozem region to the south. Rather it was felt that mechanisation would improve overall productivity by relying less on an increasing volume of labour in order to ensure higher agricultural output. At the same time, however, it was also accepted that measures had to be taken to halt the region's depopulation which, particularly as a consequence of a large exodus in the 1960s, threatened the very fabric of rural life.

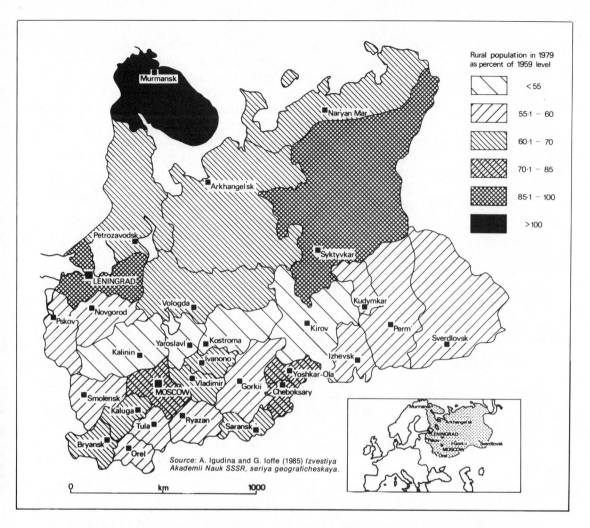

Key (Rural population in 1979 as percent of 1959 level):

- < 55
- 55·1 – 60
- 60·1 – 70
- 70·1 – 85
- 85·1 – 100
- >100

*Source:* A. Igudina and G. Ioffe (1985) *Izvestiya Akademii Nauk SSSR, seriya geograficheskaya.*

Fig. 6.1 Rural population change in the Central Non-Black Earth Zone (CNBEZ), 1959–79.

The most serious problem facing the region's development concerns its demographic decline. In the 1959–79 intercensal period, the rural population fell by 36 percent, part of a long-term trend associated with the region's urbanisation and with the better quality of life offered by local cities compared with that of their surrounding rural population. Heavy rural migration, particularly of the young, had left an ageing population structure which, due to the exodus of rural youth in particular, was unable to reproduce itself through natural population increase alone. As a consequence, a number of measures were introduced by central government to entice labour to either remain on the land or to return from the cities. The initial programme, set up in 1974, introduced a fifteen-year plan to try and revert this population decline. The scheme was directed specifically at reorganising the region's villages, many of which contained no more than twenty households. Villages well situated *vis à vis* the spartan rural transport network were to receive special long-term construction credits to build schools, kindergartens, medical services, shops, etc., while the population living in remote villages were to receive generous relocation allowances to encourage them to settle in those villages designated for development. The scheme also included an ambitious programme of providing 25,000 kilometres of hard-suface roads to connect the growth-designated villages to regional centres (Fig. 6.1). But the scheme was plagued from the outset by a number of problems. Rural road-building did not keep up with mechanisation. Due to the poor state of the roads, the large amount of capital invested in supplying the region with tractors and other machinery could not be used. Despite large investment in mechanisation, the region remained less mechanised than most other areas of the Russian republic. The programme also increased the costs of production of most crops to well above the Soviet average and to more than what the state could afford to pay collectives for their produce. But most significantly, the scheme failed to halt the exodus from the land. Between 1974 and 1981, particularly dramatic rural population decreases were recorded for the southern regions: Orel 34 percent, Kostroma 31 percent, Bryansk and Kalinin 30 percent, Tula 29 percent, Ryazan 28 percent, and Novgorod, Pskov, Yaroslavl, Gorkii and Kirov 27 percent (Perevedentsev, 1983).

As Perevedentsev (1983) has argued, the solution to the region's labour shortages cannot be met simply through increased mechanisation or by relying on retaining the available labour force. Rather, it is imperative that ways are found of attracting labour into the region. In order to encourage people living in the towns to move to the villages, since 1981 would-be migrants to the CNBEZ have been permitted to keep their town apartments for up to five years. Moreover, a number of economists and demographers have argued that a further package of material incentives to return to the land should be offered to those who have recently moved from the CNBEZ to the city, and who are therefore used to farming this particular area. Included in this scheme should be housing and generous assistance with relocation. Yet more recent measures, reminiscent of past coercive state practices, have focused on halting the rural exodus. For example, a moritorium has been introduced on employing the rural population in new job vacancies in local factories and urban industries. Restrictions on mobility between countryside and city have also been employed through the use of the passport-*propiska* system (Medvedev, 1987:406).

The CNBEZ now absorbs one-quarter of all agricultural investment but only contributes to one-sixth of output. In spite of this less than impressive performance, the region continues to be singled out for special treatment. It is still widely considered to afford the highest potential rates per ruble invested in fertilisation and land improvement and is best situated to supply the country's major urban centres. The region has also had the consistent support of conservationists, for as the historical core of ethnic Russia, the CNBEZ has long since held a special place as a symbol of the Russian way of life, which depopulation threatens. Whether the region will in the long term continue to attract large volumes of capital at the expense of rural investment in other regions when return is limited is by no means certain, yet for the time being Moscow seems prepared to take the risks involved.

*Central Asia: the river diversion project*

The environmental, economic and demographic contrasts between the CNBEZ and the predominantly Muslim republics of Central Asia could not be more extreme. Central Asia is an arid and more fertile region, with a rapidly growing rural population which has been

Water for irrigation from the Kara-Kum Canal, Turkmenistan.

reluctant to leave the countryside for the city. The region's thriving cotton economy is supported by a water supply essentially from two rivers, the Amu Darya and the Syr Darya, upon which the region's agricultural prosperity depends. Today, irrigated land comprises 97 percent of the sown area of Turkmenistan, 73 percent of Uzbekistan, 62 percent of Kirgizia, and 60 percent of Tadzhikhstan. While a considerable proportion of the region's agricultural budget goes into constructing irrigation networks, desalinising the land, and in pumping water to deserts in the south, a large amount of capital has also to be set aside each year for replacing loss of irrigated land. So in contrast to the CNBEZ, where capital has been used to substitute for labour, in Central Asia it is used to augment the agricultural area.

With growing concern in policymaking circles that the region's water resources could not continue to meet increasing demographic and economic demands, an ambitious programme was put forward in the mid-1970s to divert a portion of the north-flowing Irtysh-Ob rivers southward, to connect with a giant 2,200-kilometre-long canal, the 'Sibaral Canal', which would in turn empty into the Aral Sea (Fig. 6.2). Preliminary estimates suggested that the cost of what amounted to one of the most technically difficult projects ever envisaged by Moscow would be over 30 billion rubles.

There was considerable opposition to the project. Most of the major industrial ministries and the military were opposed to a scheme which would absorb large amounts of capital in an economy whose finance budget was having to be cut back. There was also considerable support, notably amongst agronomists, for cutting back investment in southern agriculture by giving top priority to drainage and liming in the

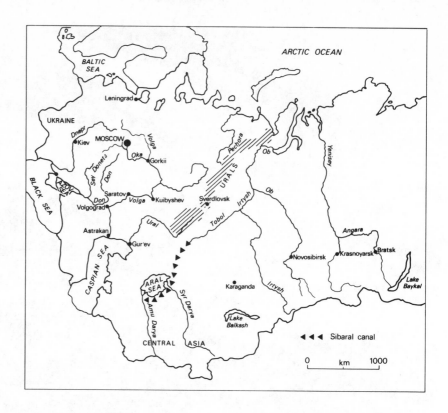

Fig. 6.2 Siberian river diversion proposals.

wet and acid areas of the European north-west. Within European USSR, vested regional and local interests cautioned against tying large amounts of capital to a project whose feasibility was questionable and which would undermine investment in the more risk-free environment of the Ukraine and the CNBEZ. The Siberian lobby was less than enthusiastic, concerned that its own large-scale, capital-intensive projects would be threatened. Environmentalists, backed up by specialists in hydrology and geography, were also concerned about the consequences such a scheme would have for maintaining Siberia's ecological balance. They also voiced their concern over the consequences the scheme might have on climates at the global scale from the effect of withdrawing such large quantities of relatively warm water from the inflow to the Arctic Ocean. Yet the Central Asian lobby, basing its argument not only on the region's growing need for ever-decreasing supplies of water but also on the contribution that such a diversion scheme could have on Central Asia's agricultural and industrial contribution to the national economy, may have actually convinced a sceptical Politburo of the long-term benefits of such an expensive project. Certainly, the region's politicians pursued an active if not always well-coordinated campaign. No doubt too, a growing awareness in Moscow of the grave problem of runaway population growth in Central Asia, particularly when contrasted with the increasing difficulty that many parts of the population of European USSR had in reproducing itself through natural population increase alone, must have lent weight to the eventual decision in 1978 to give the go-ahead to preliminary engineering and economic feasibility studies.

From the early 1980s onwards, however, two developments in particular began to undermine support for this scheme. The first concerned the extent to which available water resources in the Southlands were being put to proper use. One school had argued that additional water supplies could be made available by using present supplies more efficiently, aided by more effective reclamation programmes. The leadership in Uzbekistan was increasingly coming under fire from Moscow over their mismanagement of the region's economy. Officials were criticised for over-ambitious land reclamation schemes and for failing to take into consideration the gap between such schemes and the establishment of economically productive collective and state farms. A switch to water-conserving technologies and strict water conservation procedures rather than the past practice of putting new land into production would ensure less waste (*Pravda*, 27 July 1987). The second threat came from the state's overall commitment to large, capital-intensive projects. In order to arrest economic slowdown, it was argued, resources should be allocated to modernising existing plants and to developing industry in those regions of the economy where returns on investment would be greatest. It was the sort of overall strategy which reaffirmed a commitment at the 27th Party Congress in 1986 to further investment in the CNBEZ, but made no provision for the river diversion project. Five months later the project was officially cancelled. The project would have meant a major shift in investment priorities and a scale of commitment to Central Asia's rural development that Moscow has never before made.

Given that water shortages create surplus labour, the problem that now faces the new leadership is how to absorb this surplus into a modern economy. In the 1970–79 period, the region's population grew by 30 percent compared with 6 percent in the Russian republic. It is projected that by the year 2000, over half of all population growth will be in Muslim Central Asia. Already official estimates suggest that there are one million rural underemployed in Uzbekistan. In recognising the economic as well as the possible political ramifications of this growing army of rural surplus, a number of proposals have been put forward. While Central Asia's politicians argue for their region's industrialisation and thus job creation as the solution, many economists and demographers see the solution to reducing this growing surplus labour by encouraging migration to the labour-short cities of European USSR. Indeed, Perevedentsev (1983) has gone so far as to link a resolution to labour shortages in the CNBEZ to the labour surplus problem in Central Asia. What he proposes is that incentives should be made available, firstly to encourage recent 'discontented' migrants in Central Asia's cities (mainly Russians) to return to European USSR, so expanding urban employment opportunities in Central Asia for its rural population. Secondly, such return migration would mean that that sector of the CNBEZ labour force which has recently moved to the nearby European cities could be encouraged to move back to their native rural areas, their much-needed urban labour being in turn substituted by migrants from the south. Such an ambitious scheme would require relaxation of the passport-*propiska* system as well as considerable material relocation allowances.

## Organisational constraints and conflicts of interest

Despite greater flexibility towards regional conditions, the over-centralised organisation of rural production still remains an obstacle to higher agricultural output. The problems which arise as a consequence of rural production being largely determined 'from above', and the implications that this arrangement has for various interest groups involved in the production process, can be best illustrated by focusing on the local arena of the rural *raion*. The rural *raion* (or district) is the lowest tier in the administrative hierarchy of both government and party, and is most directly accountable to the next tier of government and party organs, the *oblast*, which in turn is responsible to the union republic and all the way up to Moscow (Fig. 6.3). Each *raion* is responsible for the collective farms within its administrative area; in turn, collective farm managers are accountable to the rural *raion*. Before we can understand the significance of these inter-relationships, it is important first to locate this local community of divergent interests within the context of the broader organisational constraints in which they operate: the procurement-price system and the role of the party in the production process.

### Procurement-price system

The system of determining what and how much the countryside should produce and the price to be paid for its produce has changed very little since its introduction in the 1930s. Both what a region has to procure for the state and the price its collective farms receive for a given product are fixed by the state. It is the function of the local party organisation as the arm of the centre in the countryside to ensure that

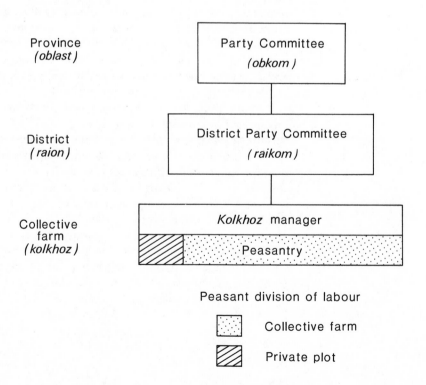

Fig. 6.3  Local party control over rural production.

Province
(oblast)

Party Committee
(obkom)

District
(raion)

District Party Committee
(raikom)

Collective farm
(kolkhoz)

Kolkhoz manager

Peasantry

Peasant division of labour

Collective farm

Private plot

the procurement quota for its local area is met by the collective farms under its jurisdiction. In the past, quota levels have been excessively high and the prices paid to collectives low.

Up until the mid-1960s, the main method of determining what and how much should be produced was based on the so-called *per hectare principle*. Compulsory delivery quotas for crop and livestock produce were simply calculated as proportionate to the farm's arable area. Provided that the rural *raikom* was able to ensure the delivery of the right product mix, collectives were then free to produce whatever additional requirements were necessary for their own consumption.

The system was very inefficient and acted as a major obstacle to regional product specialisation. Regional variations in natural conditions, labour skills, entrepreneurial activity, and the like, did not enter into the calculations. Rather, what had to be produced was the same range of products, in similar quantities, relative to total arable area. In 1964, this method of determining procurement was abandoned and replaced by the 'farm sales method' which has proved more sensitive to environmental conditions and to promoting regional specialisation. Under this method, collectives are able to deliver a quantity of products equal in *value* to that of their neighbours but not necessarily of the same mix.

In an attempt also to encourage greater efficiency and specialisation and to enable farms to operate on a more equal economic footing irrespective of natural conditions, prices paid by the state for certain products were regionalised in 1958. Since then regional price zoning has become a familiar feature of the geography of the countryside, increasing in complexity as the number of price-designated regions and products designated for regional price differentiation has grown. Such increased differentiation is an attempt to respond to the particularities of micro conditions and to move away from the lumping together of areas into large regions. For instance, after the 1976 revisions, there were 159 zones for wheat prices, compared with 15 a decade earlier. Regional price zoning has encouraged some areas to specialise because they receive higher prices for specific produce, but it has not been without its problems. This is because differentiation takes place not on the basis of differences in *conditions* facing farms (e.g. weather, labour, etc.) but on the basis of actual *costs*. Thus the most inefficient farms incur the highest costs and will be paid the highest prices irrespective of the conditions that they face. This system has also lent itself to farms growing crops which are not compatible with the natural environment because as their region has been designated a higher price region they receive a good price for producing that crop. Regional specialisation suffers under these conditions. Regions where it is potentially better to produce a commodity compatible with local natural and economic conditions have less incentive to do so.

Two recent developments to the procurement-price system are designed to provide greater flexibility. First, as part of Gorbachev's package of rural reforms, both collective and state farms are to be given the opportunity to use or sell, as they see fit, all of the produce harvested over and above the centrally-set production targets. This will enable farms to market surplus produce, the profits from which can be syphoned back into the collective. It is a scheme which has been operating in Hungary since the late 1950s and in China since 1978.

Second, since 1981 there has been a succession of increases in procurement prices. Although these increases have added substantially to the state agricultural budget, the hope is that such measures, in improving farm profitability, will also stimulate output as farms choose to reinvest their surplus into improving output, including raising wages for their employees.

### The district party organisation and the production process

One of the major debilitating effects on agriculture concerns the role that the district party organisation (the rural *raikom*) plays in the production process. It is the rural *raikom* which is responsible for ensuring that procurement targets for its district (as determined from above) are met. According to Kaplan (1983), it performs the function of 'line administrator', merely carrying out central dictats and often directly interfering in the day-to-day running of the collective farm. This, it is suggested, has a debilitating effect on agricultural production.

In the immediate post-war years, the dominance and constant meddling by the rural *raikom* in collective farm management was not helped by the lack of authority and limited skills of collective farm managers. The authority of the local party had been strengthened by a climate in which technical expertise was less important than political credentials. Devoid of much authority to make decisions, collective farm managers were not given the flexibility or autonomy to succeed, which is imperative in a sector of the economy which constantly has to make adjustments in the light of the weather. Also, few collective farm managers possessed more than a minimal education and not all were Party members, which further undermined their authority. Turnover of managers also tended to be high, no doubt symptomatic of their lack of expertise, which made it difficult to form stable contacts with other collective farm managers or with influential local party officials. Over the past three decades, however, there have been important changes which have strengthened their position. The 1950s amalgamation of collective farms has conferred considerable economic muscle on these managers; today the average *kolkhoz* has 500–600 employees and 6,200 hectares of agricultural land. Many managers are now educated in agronomy and they are usually Party members. They have also shown themselves to be a powerful pressure group as shown by the role they played in the events leading up to the abolition of the Machine Tractor Stations. In all, now that the collective farms have become gigantic enterprises equipped with modern machinery, technical and economic expertise are as important as loyalty to the Party. And yet, the pre-eminence of the Party in local production still undermines their autonomy.

This is especially so at times of 'economic crisis', when in order to ensure that regional quotas are met, the local party will intervene, typically practising 'the art of muddling through'. The following extract from a short story by Valentin Ovechkin (reproduced by Hedlund, 1984, pp. 139–40) is illustrative of this sort of practice:

Upon returning to his *raikom* after an interrupted holiday, first Party secretary Borzov finds to his dismay that, due to heavy rains, the region has fallen seriously behind the plan for grain deliveries. He is further dismayed when his second in command [Martinov] informs him that the three best *kolkhozy* in the region have already fulfilled their quotas, so that nothing more can be obtained from them. Borzov's reaction is typical . . . He then proceeds to transfer the three farms in question to the highest procurement group thereby extracting more grain from them and thus he saves the *raion* [district] procurement plan. Extremely satisfied with himself, he exclaims: 'There my boy! Don't you know how to take their grain?' Martinov objects saying that the good *kolkhozy* are being taxed extra on account of the backward ones and asks on what grounds the quotas have been increased. Borzov simply replies 'On the grounds that the country needs bread.'

So the degree of flexibility open to the farm manager is constrained owing to his accountability to the local *raikom*. As the Party requires feedback from farms on what they are capable of producing as part of the process of centrally-determined plan procurement, it is not uncommon for managers to conceal what the farm is capable of producing in order to get agreement on a low and less demanding quota. This can mean that the most productive farms purposely undersell themselves thereby contributing to planned underproduction at the farm and local level. In circumstances like this, the manager plays the role of mediator in looking after the interests of the farm members (the peasantry) while satisfying what is expected of the farm by the local Party. In acknowledging such practices, the 1986 Party Congress advocated greater independence and initiative to collective and state farms; how this will affect relations between farm managers and the local Party has yet to be seen.

## The peasant household and 'the private economy'

The nature of the collective farm furnishes its members with a sense of communal consciousness. Its institutional framework provides a means of direct member participation in its day-to-day running while its services and amenities furnish a focal point for the community's economic and cultural life. Undermining this sense of collective consciousness is a daily system of work practices in which the peasantry divide their labour between their obligations to the collective farm and their household. It is a delicate balance which brings them into conflict with collective farm managers concerned with meeting production targets.

The peasantry have certain mandatory obligations to the collective. They have to work an agreed minimum number of hours per week for which, from only as recently as 1966, they receive a guaranteed minimum wage. Having fulfilled these obligations to the collective, they are then free to work on their private plot.

An important concession from collectivisation for peasant households was the right to a private plot. The produce from this, after family needs are met, can also be sold on the open market. The private plot supplies virtually all the household's food requirements. But it also supplements the low income from the collective. In Belorussia, for instance, 40 percent of peasant income is derived from the private plot. As for the state, it has long since hesitated over the most appropriate policy to adopt towards such small-scale private farming. Over recent years, however, greater tolerance has prevailed, the official view being that with growth in the output of collective farms and resulting higher wages, the need for private agriculture will disappear. Yet in spite of its activities being subject to strict regulation, more recent policy statements view it as having a definite place. 'Private subsidiary food production', according to Brezhnev, 'should receive more attention, more concern', a view also held by the current leadership. That a benevolent attitude should prevail is primarily due to economic expediency. Today, just over a quarter of all agricultural production comes from the private plot, even though it only accounts for 3 percent of the total agricultural area. It is especially important for dairy produce, vegetables and market gardening, and produces more than 50 percent of the country's potatoes and vegetables. In short, the private plot plays an appreciable role in making good the shortfalls in the collective farm system; it also provides a variety in diet which society has grown to expect.

Unlike work on the collective farm, there is a direct relationship between effort put into the private plot, and reward. Collective farm managers, having to ensure that production quotas are met, set high quotas on the hours to be spent mandatorily on the collective in order that too much time is not devoted to the private plot. This has had a number of consequences. First, the peasantry are forced to forfeit more of their leisure time in order to secure subsistence. Second, it has led to the problem of absenteeism from the collective farm, particularly at harvest time when perishables cannot wait upon the demands of the procurement system. Third and more generally, it has contributed to lower productivity on the collective farm as peasants resent how their time budgets are being organised without acknowledgement of effort.

In recognising such a conflict of interest, the state has responded not by attacking the private plot but rather by introducing greater flexibility of work on the collective farm. This has involved broadening the use of the effort-rewarding *zveno* system. It operates by encouraging groups of workers to form teams of between three and ten members who take out contracts with a collective farm. These teams, each free to select its own members, are paid by results on top of their guaranteed minimum wage. Yields obtained are thus personalised. It is a form of labour organisation well-suited to intensive farming, and one which is now widely practised with considerable success.


## Agro-industrial complexes

One of the longstanding aims of the USSR has been to erase the economic and social differences which separate town from country. As the country has matured industrially, and as the countryside has generated its own agriculturally-based industrial activities (e.g. food-processing plants), and makes greater demands on urban-based industries for its products (e.g. chemical fertilisers), planners have increasingly recognised that in the interests of improving agricultural performance, there is a need to establish an organisation to coordinate these activities.

The idea of an agro-industrial complex is not new. The notion of integrating agricultural activities into a more complex agro-industrial cycle was included in the 1961 programme. It was not, however, until 1978, after some experimentation in Estonia, that it was finally decided to set up a system of organisation to administer this agro-industrial cycle as a whole. It is now pivotal to the process of rural production and distribution (Lemeshev, 1985). In most respects, the agro-industrial complex (*agrano-promyshlennyi kompleks*) has a similar logic to the territorial production complex (see chapter 4). The various 'agencies' involved in the production and distribution process are organisationally integrated, so breaking down the bureaucratic barriers between agencies, especially between 'sectoral' and 'local' organisations. It is also intended to be more sensitive to 'local needs'. For example, one of the problems that both collective and state farms faced was that on a day-to-day basis they had to deal with a range of different ministries. Thus if a collective farm required fertilisers, these were obtained from one ministry; for the purchase or repair of machinery it had to deal with another; it could not carry out land reclamation without financial support from yet another. In turn produce had to be delivered to different procurement ministries (e.g. meat and milk had to be delivered to the plants belonging to the Meat and Milk Industry, grain to the Ministry of Procurement, Potato and Cabbage, and so forth). The intention then was to set up a system of organisation to ensure greater coordination between these agencies which would improve agricultural specialisation and efficiency.

In order to coordinate the various activities of the agro-industrial complex, a geographically nested hierarchy of agro-industrial organisations was established. At the most local level is the *raion*-based organisation, RAPO (an acronym for *raionnoye agro-promyshelnnoye ob'edinenye*); it brings together a number of agencies and organisations including collective and state farms, inter-farm production units, the district units, and a wide-ranging number of ministries (e.g. Agriculture, Procurements, Meat and Milk, Food, Land Reclamation). Their main aim is to coordinate work on increasing agricultural production, using funds rationally, and on improving mechanisation and technical services. In bringing collective and state farms into the decision-making process, the hope is that the bureaucratic problems that these enterprises faced with their dealings with the above ministries, would be lessened. There is every indication to suggest that RAPO has succeeded in opening up debate and discussion between the various agencies and their locally-based ministerial representatives, and that the ministries are more aware of the administrative and day-to-day problems faced in running collective and state farms. Yet as an organisation its activities are circumscribed by vested ministerial interests as well as by *oblast*-level interests and those further up the organisational hierarchy. To this end, the establishment in 1985 of a new 'super ministry' of agriculture (*Gosagroprom*), which replaces most of the ministries responsible for various activities in the agricultural sector, certainly simplifies the decision-making process and the bureaucracy. It is clearly a reform which should make the running of agro-industrial complexes easier.

## Differences between town and country

The aim of working towards the removal of social and economic differences between countryside and city remains an important goal. The further integration of the rural economy and its settlement structure with that of the city now forms an important basis of policy towards the countryside and is seen as a means of improving rural economic performance and standards of living.

The restructuring of the rural settlement system is accepted as a vital way of improving the quality of life and economic efficiency of rural areas, and of furthering the integration of town and countryside. Policymakers and planners have been particularly concerned with designing a rural settlement network which will slow down rural depopulation and resolve consequential labour shortages in the countryside. To this end, collectivisation was an important process in consolidating the rural population into larger and eventually better-serviced villages. But it has been particularly 'the residue' of the rural settlement network – those small and remote villages and settlements which have been generally left behind by the territorial reorganisation of the countryside – which have been the subject of much concern. Today many of these villages suffer from inadequate service provision and from a poor rural transport network to often distant centres of production. In an attempt to improve overall standards of living through more effective service provision, the policy has been to distinguish between 'viable' and 'non-viable' villages; the former, usually the larger villages, receive generous inputs of capital in order to enable the more effective provision of services and amenities, as well as greater diversity of employment, particularly in industries connected with rural production (i.e. agro-industrial complexes). Those smaller villages designated as non-viable are purposely starved of investment and their inhabitants encouraged through a variety of material incentives to resettle in those villages earmarked as growth centres. It is a scheme which forms an integrated approach to planning the settlement system as a unitary whole and which takes into consideration the relationships and inter-dependencies between places, from the large city right down to the small village. Inter-dependence and functional differentiation therefore provide the basis for a policy of providing a comprehensive range of accessible services and amenities and a wider range of employment opportunities for the rural population.

While the problem of rural depopulation remains, in part a symptom of the lower standards of service provision and employment prospects in the countryside, there would seem to be little doubt that a more integrated system of settlement planning has aided in bringing what urbanism has to offer closer to the countryside. As Strongina (1978) notes, 'urbanisation becomes an important factor in the transformation of settlement throughout the nation'. Many Soviet planners remain sceptical of the long-term benefit to the countryside of the modernising influence of the urban way of life and of the consequences it has for the peasant culture and traditions. Yet rural living standards have improved immeasurably, but still significant differences remain. This can be illustrated in terms of education and income.

In terms of education, the most recent census data show that 25 out of every 1,000 rural inhabitants have a higher education compared with 93 for every 1,000 city dwellers. Income differentials also remain but the significance of the peasant private plot inflates rural wages which account for about a quarter of the collective farmers' income. However, one of the most striking similarities is the way in which income is spent, and here there has been a marked convergence as urban-consumer life styles have disseminated into the countryside. In 1981, 76 out of every 100 rural families had television and 78 per 100 radios (compared with 95 and 93 per 100 urban families respectively). While the cultural impact of urban values on the countryside is great, peasants still spend far less on services and on cultural amenities per household than urban industrial workers do.

The persistence of variation in opportunities which such differences between town and country still represent make it that much more difficult to encourage the young in particular to remain in the countryside. The internal passport, as we have noted, has in the past helped to regulate such an exodus from rural areas, but as a consequence of its gradual introduction to the previously disenfranchised peasantry over the 1976–80 period, it has made it easier to villagers to leave and take up urban employment. Exodus from the countryside has also been made easier as a consequence of Gorbachev's reforms which include granting the peasantry the right to leave the collective farm without permission. However, it would seem that without substantially improving living and working conditions in the countryside, rural out-migration is likely to undermine the prospects for a more buoyant rural economy in the future.

# 7  Conclusions

The Soviet Union's experience of development presents a mixed picture of both substantial achievement and significant shortfalls. In this book it has been argued that in order to understand the Soviet Union of today and its achievements and problems, it is vital to locate its development within an historical context. We have singled out the Stalinist model for development as being especially critical in understanding the making of Soviet society and how it contrasts with other experiences of development in both socialist and non-socialist countries. While the Stalinist legacy of combined and uneven development has left an indelible imprint, it is also evident that considerable changes have occurred since the mid-1950s to the territorial organisation of Soviet society and to the nature and conduct of politics. It is within such a context of wrestling with the legacy of the past and with the social and economic problems arising from a more urbanised and industrialised society, that more recent generations of Soviet policymakers have had to address themselves.

It is important not to underestimate what has actually been achieved in a remarkably short period. Within seventy years, the Soviet Union has moved from being a poor and backward country to one of the world's most industrialised and urbanised countries. In 1928, Soviet Gross Domestic Product was roughly one-quarter that of the United States; by 1980, the ratio had risen to three-quarters. No country has matched the speed at which the USSR industrialised, and only Japan has rivalled the Soviet long-term growth record. The Soviet Union's military capability and global influence is now second only to that of the United States. While there is no doubt that the priorities of centralised planning have both accelerated the growth rates of industrial output and ensured the continuing high spending on defence, improvements in the quality of life and in overall living standards have been far from neglected. The population is measurably far better off than it was thirty years ago. Moreover, in the process of becoming a fully urban-industrial society, the state has avoided the pitfalls of large-scale unemployment which have plagued other countries of the non-socialist world. There has, however, been a high price to pay for such achievements.

We noted in chapter 2 that rapid and extensive industrialisation was purchased at the expense of the Soviet people. Both urban and rural living standards were affected as a result of the preoccupation with industrial production and defence. Consequently, compared with industrialised Western countries, the average Soviet consumer has a lower standard of living. Moreover, as one highly respected Soviet sociologist, Zaslavskaya, recently noted, 'the organs of government in recent years have not by any means always been able to maintain a genuine planned socio-economic development of society' (1986:64).

That geographical imbalances persist can be attributed to three main causes:

1  Spatial efficiency combined with the powers of the highly centralised industrial ministries and the nature of sectoral planning have continued to favour the development of some regions over others. This is not to deny the significant strides that have been made in the economic development of Siberia and Central Asia but merely to point out that prioritising economic growth has worked against more balanced regional development.

2  Extensive industrialisation, which puts a low premium on social infrastructural investment (e.g. housing), has resulted in underurbanisation and the consequent emergence of a disadvantaged group of commuters. In attempting to cope with housing shortages and overburdened city services, the passport-*propiska* system has not only exacerbated labour shortages in 'closed cities', but by regulating social and geographical mobility into these privileged places, has contributed to social inequality.

3  The territorially overcentralised nature of the Soviet Union and of its major economic and political institutions has resulted in limiting the scope of the regions and cities in running their own affairs. Overcentralisation and the sectoral management of the economy has also worked against their more effectively planned coordination and development, while a lack of sensitivity to the particularities of local conditions and problems (at all geographical levels) has often been detrimental to production and to the well-being of communities.

This, however, is only part of the picture. The period of rapid industrial growth has long since ended. The growth rate of the country's GNP had fallen from 6 percent per annum in the early 1950s to a rate somewhere between 2 and 3 percent by the 1980s. Part of the reason for this fall is due to the Soviet Union's difficulty of effectively moving from an extensive to an intensive growth economy; that is, growth based upon increases in efficiency rather than upon the growth of factor inputs (i.e. capital and labour). It is precisely a recognition of the need to resuscitate an ailing Soviet economy combined with greater concern with fulfilling socialism's expectations of social justice and equality, which have resulted in the emergence of a new programme for Soviet development, based on the notion of *perestroika*.

### *Perestroika:* a new beginning?

We noted in chapter 4 the possible impact of *perestroika* on the regions. As for its broader implications for a new geography of planned development, three aspects are particularly central.

Firstly, the Gorbachev leadership recognises that national economic growth has been sluggish owing to the ineffectiveness of past governments in modernising production and in using investment capital more expediently in order to maximise returns. It has therefore set itself the goal of increasing the variety and quality of capital and consumer items, partly in order to make Soviet manufacturing goods more competitive within a world economy. As we noted in chapter 4, the updating of industrial plants and equipment has been singled out for special attention, linked to which is the more effective use of research and development. Investment capital is also to be geared towards those sectors of the economy where it will produce the highest economic returns. Capital-intensive projects, many associated with the further development of Siberia and Central Asia, have either been abandoned or are to receive a lower priority. It would therefore seem that European USSR is likely to continue to benefit from such a development strategy, which may well be at the cost of some of the country's less developed regions.

Secondly, more effective use is to be made of the labour force. We noted in chapters 3 and 4 that labour shortages, particularly acute in parts of European USSR and Siberia, act as a brake to further development. But the regime not only recognises that there is a population distribution problem, in which ways of attracting labour to areas of shortfall have to be improved, but that further measures have to be introduced in order to use it more efficiently. For example, as Zaslavskaya (1986:62) notes with concern, 'the existence of job vacancies in most regions and cities makes it possible in principle for people to earn quite handsomely without over-exerting themselves. Characteristically, 27 percent of managers of industrial enterprises in the Altai region [of Southern Siberia] consider the strained labour situation and the "competition" between enterprises for labour to be the principal reason why the work force is not more active'. Among the many steps taken to improve labour productivity (including greater worker participation in the running of industrial enterprises and stamping out worker absenteeism), are measures designed to retrain and relocate workers in those sectors of the economy and in administration which are overmanned. In Moscow, for example, it has

Considerable upheaval for the labour force has accompanied the reorganisation of large bureaucracies as a result of *perestroika*. For many administrative-managerial personnel in cities like Moscow, it means changing jobs, retraining or moving to another city. Here, the Ministry of Higher and Specialised Secondary Education becomes part of a new USSR State Commission on People's Education.

been estimated that as a consequence of 'restructuring', a third of the city's administrative and managerial personnel will lose their jobs. While the intention is to reabsorb through 'retraining' a large proportion of this 'surplus' labour back into the city economy (notably through newly set-up cooperatives), it is also recognised that many will have to move elsewhere to find employment. But the problem of the *propiska* remains a stumbling block to encouraging resettlement for there is no guarantee of housing and a place of residence permit to those wishing to return eventually to their native 'closed city', something which a number of prominent reformers accept must change (*Pravda*, 21 January 1988).

Finally, measures have also been announced to decentralise many aspects of economic and political decision-making to the regions, cities and workplaces. The territorially-based soviets in particular, are to have more say in the running of their own affairs, which is designed to make the overall decision-making process more accountable to the Soviet citizen. These reforms are clearly attractive to territorial organisations – such as the union republics and town soviets – whose power to influence the more rounded development of their own communities has in the past been heavily circumscribed by the centre. Yet the essential characteristics and features of central planning and of the agencies, like the industrial ministries, who have a vested interest in maintaining the centralised character of planned development, still remain intact. It is likely that into the foreseeable future this territorial dimension – between those agencies favouring the continuing territorial centralisation of power and concentration of resources, and those favouring the devolution of power and resource deconcentration – will remain a central ingredient to the politics of development.

# Glossary

The following Russian terms and abbreviations have been used in the text.

**CMEA**   Council for Mutual Economic Assistance (or Comecon), the form of economic alliance between Soviet bloc countries.
**CNBEZ**   Central Non-Black Earth Zone.
**FYP**   Five Year Plan.
**Goskomtrud**   State Commission for Labour and Social Problems.
**Gosplan**   State Planning Committee.
**GULag**   the prison and labour camp network in the Soviet Union.
**kolkhoz**   collective farm.
**kolkhozniki**   collective farm members (or peasantry).
**Komsomol**   Young Communist League, the mass movement to which the majority of young people belong.
**kulak**   a well-to-do peasant.
**limitchiki or 'limit workers'**   workers brought into a large city and issued with temporary residence permits.
**MTS**   Machine Tractor Stations.
**NEP**   New Economic Policy.
**oblast**   major administrative subdivision, comparable to a province.
**obkom**   provincial party committee at the *oblast* level.
**Orgnabor**   the scheme for the organised recruitment of labour.
**perestroika**   the policy of restructuring.
**Politburo**   the top decision-making body in the Soviet Union.
**propiska**   a residence permit.
**raikom**   Party committee in a *raion*.
**raion**   administrative subdivision of an *oblast*, meaning 'district'.
**soviet**   the Russian word for 'council', the basic governmental unit of the Soviet system.
**Sovetskii narod**   the Soviet people.
**sovnarkhoz**   regional economic council.
**sovkhoz**   state farm.
**TPC**   Territorial Production Complex.
**tukhta**   the practice of padding production reports.
**USSR**   Union of Soviet Socialist Republics.
**union republic**   major administrative unit; there are fifteen of them, each based on a major nationality homeland.
**zveno**   small group of agricultural workers.

# Bibliography and further reading

The following sources have been used in writing this book. An asterisk indicates suggested further reading.

**Chapter 1**

**Bideleux, R.** (1985) *Communism and Development*, Methuen, London.
*****Forbes, D. and Thrift, N.** (eds) (1987) *The Socialist Third World. Urban development and territorial planning*, Blackwell, Oxford.
**Hough, J.** (1972) 'The Soviet system: petrification or pluralism?', *Problems of communism* 2, 25–45.
**Lenin, V. I.** (1963) *Polnoe sobranie sochinenii, Piatoe izdanie*, vol. 23, Moscow.
**Murray, P. and Szelenyi, I.** (1984) 'The city in the transition to socialism', *International Journal of Urban and Regional Research* 8(1), 90–107.
*****Pallot, J. and Shaw, D.** (1981) *Planning in the Soviet Union*, Croom Helm, London.
*****Shaw, D.** *et al.* (1990) *The Soviet Union. Geography of an administered society*, Longman, London.
**White, S.** (1983) 'What is a communist system?', *Studies in Comparative Communism* 16(4), 247–63.
**Whyte, M. and Parish, W.** (1984) *Urban Life in Contemporary China*, University of Chicago Press, Chicago.

**Chapter 2**

**Barsov, A. A.** (1969) *Balans stroimostnykh obmenov mezhdu gorodom i derevney*, Nauka, Moscow.
**Davies, R.** (1978) 'Industrialisation and after' in R. Davies (ed.) *The Soviet Union*, Allen and Unwin, London.
**Gregory, P. and Stuart, R.** (1986) *Soviet Economic Structure and Performance*, Harper & Row, New York.
**Lorimer, F.** (1946) *The Population of the Soviet Union. History and prospects*, League of Nations, Geneva.
**Millar, J. and Nove, A.** (1976) 'A debate on Soviet collectivisation. Was Stalin really necessary?', *Problems of Communism* July/August, 49–62.
**Rashin, A. G.** (1956) *Naselenie Rossii za 100 let*, Gosudarstvennoe Statisticheskoe Izdatel'stvo, Moscow.
**Rosefielde, S.** (1980) 'The first "Great Leap Forward" reconsidered: lessons of Solzhenitsyn's Gulag Archipelago', *Slavic Review* 39(4), 560–87.
*****Wheatcroft, S. G.** *et al.* (1986) 'Soviet industrialisation reconsidered: some preliminary conclusions about economic development between 1926 and 1941', *Economic History Review* 39(2), 264–94.

**Chapter 3**

**Bialkovskaya, V. and Novikov, V.** (1982) 'Urbanizatsiya i problemy organicheniya rosta krupneishikh gorodov', *Voprosy Ekonomiki* 11, 89–98.
**Gor'kovskaya Pravda**, 22 June 1984.
**Khorev, B.** (1984) 'Aktual'nye nachno-prikladnye problemy organicheniya rosta krupnykh gorodov v SSSR', *Ekonomicheskie Nauki* 3, 60–8.
*****Nechemias, C.** (1981) 'The impact of Soviet housing policy on housing conditions in Soviet cities: the uneven push from Moscow', *Urban Studies* 18, 1–8.

**Ogonyok** No. 5, January 1987.

**Pravda** 21 January 1985.

**Ross, C.** (1986) *Local government in the Soviet Union*, Croom Helm, London.

***Rowland, R. H.** (1983) 'The growth of large cities in the USSR: policies and trends', *Urban Geography* 4(3), 258–79.

**Shelley, L.** (1984) 'Urbanisation and crime: the Soviet experience', in *H. Morton and R. Stuart (eds) *The Contemporary Soviet City*, Macmillan, New York, pp. 113–28.

**Sigov, I.** (1986) 'Nastoiashchee i budushchee krupnykh gorodov', *Voprosy Ekonomiki* 3, 44–51.

***Smith, G. E.** (1989) 'Privilege and place in Soviet society', in D. Gregory and R. Walford (eds) *Horizons in Human Geography*, Macmillan, London.

**Sobesednik** No. 7, February 1987.

**Sotsialisticheskaya industria** 25 March 1987.

**Stanislavskii, A.** (1974) 'Tempy razvitiya krupneishchikh gorodov UKSSR i zadachi regulirovaniya ikh rosta', in A. Stanislavskii *et al.*, *Problemy Ekonomiki Gradastroitel'stva*, Kiev.

**Trube, L. L.** (1985) 'Pochemu ne udaetsiya salezhat rost krupnykh gorodov?', *Sotsiologicheskie Issledovaniya* 1, 90–2.

**Zaslavskaya, T.** (1970) *Migratsiya Sel'skogo Naselenia*, Moscow.


## Chapter 4

**Bandman, M.** (ed.) (1976) *Regional Development in the USSR. Modelling the formation of Soviet territorial production complexes*, Pergamon, Oxford.

**Barabasheva, I.** (1980) 'Upravelenie territorial'noe proizvodstvennym kompleksam (TPK)', *Sovetskoe Gosudarstvo i Pravo* 5, pp. 00.

***Bond, A.** (1987) 'Spatial dimensions of Gorbachev's economic strategy', *Soviet Geography*, 28(7), 490–523.

***Dellenbrant, J. A.** (1986) *The Soviet Regional Dilemma. Planning, people and natural resources*, M. E. Sharpe, London.

***Dienes, L.** (1987) 'Regional planning and the development of Soviet Asia', *Soviet Geography* 287–310.

**Izvestiya** 30 June 1986, 7.

**Nozdrina, N.** (1982) 'Migratsionnye protsessy v raione Kansko-Achinskogo toplivno-energeticheskogo kompleksa', *Sotsiologicheskie Issledovanniya* 1, 90–3.

**Perevedentsev, V.** (1982) 'Vospeoizvodstvo naseleniya i sem'ya', *Sotsiologicheskii Issledovaniya* 2, 80–8.

**Pravda** 12 June 1985.

**Rumer, B.** (1984) *Investment and Reindustrialisation in the Soviet economy*, Westview, Boulder.

**Shirokova, L. and Mosina, L.** (1982) 'Rayonnoe, regulirovanie zarabotnoy platy', *Organizatsiya Promyshlennogo Proizvodstva* 2, 105–16.

***Smith, G. E.** (1983) 'Rethinking Soviet population policy', *Area* 15(2), 137–43.

**Zaslavskaya, V., Kalmyk, V. and Khakhulina, L.** (1986) 'Problemy sotsial'nogo razvitiya Sibiri puti ikh resheniya', *Izvestiya Sibirskogo otdeleniya Akademii nauk SSSR. Seriya ekonomiki i prikladnoi sotsiologii* 1, 36–45.


## Chapter 5

**Bahry, D.** (1987) *Outside Moscow. Power, politics, and budgetary policy in the Soviet republics*, Columbia University Press, New York.

***Clem, R.** (1987) 'The ethnic dimension', in J. Pankhurst and M. Sacks (eds), *Contemporary Soviet Society*, Praeger, New York.

***Gorbachev, M.** (1987) *Perestroika. New thinking for our society and the world*, Collins, London.

**Jones, E. and Grupp, F.** (1984) 'Modernisation and ethnic equalisation in the USSR', *Soviet Studies* 36(2), 159–84.

**Pravda** 26 February 1986.

**Pravda** 9 February 1988.

Rudzat, Ya. Ya. and Vitolins, E. K. (1977) 'Latviiskaya Sovetskaya Sotsialisticheskaya Respublika', in T. V. Ryabushkin (ed.) *Naseline Soyuznykh Respublik*, Moscow.

Smith, G. E. (1989) 'Administering ethnoregional stability. The Soviet state and the nationalities problem', in C. Williams and E. Kofman (eds) *Community Conflict, Partition and Nationalism*, Routledge, London, pp. 224–50.

*Smith, G. E. (1989) 'Gorbachev's greatest challenge : *perestroika* and the national question', *Political Geography Quarterly* 8(1), 7–20.

Wallerstein, I. (1973) 'The two modes of ethnic consciousness: Soviet Central Asia in transition', in E. Allworth (ed.) *The Nationality Question in Soviet Central Asia*, Praeger, New York.

Zwick, P. (1979) 'Ethnoregional socio-economic fragmentation and Soviet budgetary policy', *Soviet Studies* 31(3), 380–400.

## Chapter 6

*Gustafson, T. (1981) *Reform in Soviet Politics. Lessons of recent policies on land and water*, Cambridge University Press, Cambridge.

Hedlund, S. (1984) *Crisis in Soviet Agriculture*, Croom Helm, London.

Kaplan, C. (1983) 'The Communist Party of the Soviet Union and local policy implementation', *Journal of Politics* 45(1), 2–27.

Kerblay, B. (1983) *Modern Soviet Society*, Methuen, London.

Lemeshev, M. (1985) 'Prodovol'stvennaia programma i okhrana okruzhaiushchei sredy', *Voprosy Ekonomiki* 12, 79–89.

*Medvedev, Z. (1987) *Soviet Agriculture*, W. Norton & Co., London.

Perevedentsev, V. I. (1983) 'Migratsiya naseleniya i razvitie sel'skokhoziastvennogo proizvodstva', *Sotsialogicheskie Issledovaniya* I, 54–61.

Pravda 12 June 1985.

Pravda 27 July 1987.

Sinyuva, M. (1980) *Nechernozömnaya RSFSR. Ekonomicheskie problemy razvitia selskogo khozyaista*, Moscow.

Strongina, M. (1978) 'Razvitie i regulirovanie sistem rasseleniya', *Voprosy Ekonomiki* 12, 55–65.

## Chapter 7

Pravda 21 January 1988.

Zaslavskaya, T. (1986) 'Chelovecheskii faktor razvitiia ekonomiki i sotsial'naia spravedlivost', *Kommunist* 13, 61–73.

*The following statistical sources have been used throughout the text:*

Tsentral'noe Statistcheskoe Upravlenie pri Sovete Ministrov SSSR (1962) *Itogi Vsesoyuznoi Perepisi Naseleniya 1959 goda*, Moscow.

Tsentral'noe Statisticheskoe Upravlenie pri Sovete Ministrov SSSR (1972–73) *Itogi Vsesoyuznoi Perepisi Naseleniya 1970 goda*, Moscow.

Tsentral'noe Statisticheskoe Upravlenie SSSR (1980) *Naselenie SSSR. Po dannym vsesoyuznoi perepisi naseleniya 1979 goda*, Izdatel'stvo politicheskoi literatury, Moscow.

Tsentral'noe Statisticheskoe Upravlenie SSSR (for various years) Narodnoe Khozyaistvo SSSR, Moscow.

Vestnik Statistiki, 1980–88.

World Bank (1987) *World Development Report 1987*, Oxford University Press, Oxford.

# Index